THOMAS AQUINAS
FOR BEGINNERS

Thomas Aquinas for Beginners

A Brief Introduction to His Philosophy

Jeffrey E. Coleman

Sapientia Press
of Ave Maria University

Copyright 2012 by Sapientia Press of Ave Maria University, Naples, FL.
All rights reserved.

No part of this publication may be reproduced or transmitted in any form or means, electronic or mechanical, including photography, recording, or any other information storage or retrieval system, without permission in writing from the publisher.

Requests for permission to make copies of any part of the work should be directed to:

Sapientia Press
of Ave Maria University
5050 Ave Maria Blvd.
Ave Maria, Florida 34142
888-343-8607

Cover Image: *Saint Thomas Aquinas*, Elsheimer, Adam (c.1574–1610).

Photo Credit: John Hammond.
National Trust Photo Library/Art Resource, NY

Printed in the United States of America.

Library of Congress Control Number: 2012934764

ISBN: 978-1-932589-62-7

CONTENTS

Introduction vii

CHAPTER ONE — God 1

CHAPTER TWO — Man 27

CHAPTER THREE — Ethics: Happiness and Virtue 35

CHAPTER FOUR — Law 57

Glossary 79
Further Reading 83
Index 85

INTRODUCTION

This book was written for those who would like a brief and non-technical introduction to the philosophy of St. Thomas Aquinas. Short selections are taken from Aquinas's most famous work, the *Summa theologiae* (Summary of Theology). Then, a commentary explaining each selected passage is given. For the sake of brevity and clarity, not every article in the *Summa* has been included in this book. The best way to read the book is to read the selection from Aquinas, earnestly trying to understand him on his own terms, and only then to turn to the commentary for further light. The hope is that some of his most important philosophical insights will emerge from such a study.

But why would anyone want to know about philosophy anyway? Well, some people have heard of philosophy but have only a vague knowledge of what it is all about and would like to know more. Moreover, for Christians, many of the religious concepts they are used to hearing are intimately bound up with philosophy, ideas such as the Trinity and the Incarnation, which employ or include philosophical notions such as "nature" and "substance." Knowing more about philosophy, then, strengthens the foundation on which one's Christian Faith is built; as Aquinas is fond of saying, just as grace builds on nature, so faith builds on natural knowledge and does not contradict it.[1]

Furthermore, Pope John Paul II in his encyclical *Fides et Ratio* (Faith and Reason), which concerns the importance of philosophy, writes: "The

---

[1] For example, see below at I, q. 2, a. 2, ad 1 (part I, question 2, article 2, reply to objection 1).

truths of philosophy, it should be said, are not restricted only to the sometimes ephemeral teachings of professional philosophers. All men and women, as I have noted, are in some sense philosophers and have their own philosophical conceptions with which they direct their lives. In one way or other, they shape a comprehensive vision and an answer to the question of life's meaning, and in the light of this they interpret their own life's course and regulate their behavior " (§30). In other words, one cannot avoid having a philosophy, and so, one ought to try to make sure that that philosophy is true and not riddled with confusion and error. At least some study of philosophy, therefore, is in order, and a good place to start is under the tutelage of St. Thomas Aquinas.

LIFE OF ST. THOMAS AQUINAS (1225–1274)

Thomas Aquinas was the son of a wealthy nobleman and was expected to embark upon an ecclesiastical career that would bring his family more power and prestige, possibly as the Benedictine abbot of Monte Cassino. Instead, Thomas decided to join the relatively new mendicant (begging) religious order begun by St. Dominic (1170–1221), the Order of Preachers (or Dominicans). His family fought his decision but eventually gave way to his unshakeable determination. The Dominicans quickly realized how intelligent Thomas was, so, once he had finished his education, he took the prestigious Dominican chair of theology at the University of Paris, the intellectual center of Christendom at the time. The particular Dominican ideal is to contemplate God and then to share the fruits of one's contemplation with others through teaching and preaching (and, of course, through good example). Aquinas was an excellent example of this; he was a Christian theologian open to truth from any source, even pagan sources such as the great Greek philosopher Aristotle (384–322 B.C.). Some theologians in his day thought that allowing Aristotle (most preferred Plato) to play a role in one's theological speculation was dangerous, since Aristotle seemed to teach some things that are contrary to the Christian Faith. But Aquinas recognized that allowing truth from any quarter into one's own system—and he drew from everybody available to him, for example: Aristotle; Plato and his followers, the Neoplatonists; St. Augustine; and Jewish and Islamic thinkers—would only

INTRODUCTION

enrich one's thinking. It therefore became a matter, in the case of Aristotle, for instance, of trying to understand what exactly he was saying, taking—and sometimes transforming in the light of Christian revelation—what was good and true, and correcting what was false.

For Aquinas, if a conclusion in philosophy contradicted a truth of the Faith, he knew that that was a matter of bad philosophy putting forth a false conclusion; he allowed the Christian Faith to serve as a corrective to bad philosophy and taught the harmony of faith and reason as both having their source in God. In contrast, some contemporaries of Aquinas, called Radical Aristotelians, taught that correct philosophy could contradict the Faith, even if in the end they sided with the Faith; their position allowed that the two realms of faith and reason could exist in a state of conflict. For instance, even though they would have held by faith that the world began a finite time ago (as taught by the Book of Genesis), they also held that reason could establish that the world did not have a beginning in time but always existed. That way of viewing the relationship between faith and reason was foreign to Aquinas, whose synthesis of philosophy and theology was very rich indeed, evidenced by repeated endorsements of his way of thinking by recent Roman Catholic popes, starting with Leo XIII (pope from 1878–1903), who started a Thomistic revival, and lasting to our own day with John Paul II and Benedict XVI.[2]

Now, the articles of the *Summa* dealt with here constitute only a tiny fraction of the thousands of articles that make up that monumental work. And the *Summa* is itself only one of Aquinas's many works of philosophy and theology. So please avail yourself of the suggested reading list at the end of the book and go on from there to the works that they

---

[2] John Paul II writes in *Fides et Ratio*, §44: "Profoundly convinced that 'whatever its source, truth is of the Holy Spirit' (*omne verum a quocumque dicatur a Spiritu Sancto est*) St. Thomas was impartial in his love of truth. He sought truth wherever it might be found and gave consummate demonstration of its universality. In him, the Church's Magisterium has seen and recognized the passion for truth; and precisely because it stays consistently within the horizon of universal, objective and transcendent truth, his thought scales 'heights unthinkable to human intelligence.' Rightly, then, he may be called an 'apostle of the truth.'" Moreover, Benedict XVI speaks admiringly of St. Thomas in his General Audience of June 2, 2010.

suggest. But always remember that even though Aquinas was a brilliant thinker, the bedrock fact about him was his faith and his love of God. Above all, he desired God, and he now enjoys the presence of God in heaven. All of his teaching, all of his writing, all of his effort was directed toward the knowledge and the love of God, as well as the hope that he could pass on to others all that God was so gracious to give to him.

This fundamental truth is reflected in the overall structure of the *Summa theologiae*, which some commentators have interpreted as involving an *exitus-reditus* scheme, *exitus* and *reditus* being the Latin words for "exit" and "return," respectively. In other words, the *Summa* starts with God, then moves to God's creation, including the pinnacle of creation, man; then it's on to man's return to God, which is the concern of ethics and law. Ultimately, of course, it is Jesus Christ Who is "the Way" back to God for man, and if this were a theology book, we would go on to cover what Aquinas has to say about Christ and His gift of the sacraments. In any case, this idea of "exit-return" can help us understand what Aquinas and the *Summa* are all about.

Note on Reading the *Summa Theologiae* of St. Thomas

Aquinas writes the *Summa* in the form of disputed questions, which was a common way to write, teach, and learn in medieval times. So, he begins by asking a question, then proceeds to state objections to what will be his opinion. Then, there's an "On the contrary" section that usually goes against the objections and cites an authority, often the Bible (quotations from which Aquinas would have taken from the Vulgate edition). At that point, Aquinas gives his own answer to the question in the "I answer that" section. Finally, after his reply, he responds to the initial objections.[3] Then he moves on to the next question. This should help to dispel any confusion about the form in which Aquinas writes the *Summa*. All of the sections in italic type below are the words of Aquinas.

---

[3] Nearly every article in the *Summa* has these main features, but not all of these features have been included here for the sake of brevity and clarity.

CHAPTER ONE

GOD

I, q. 1, a. 1
(which means part I, question 1, article 1)

QUESTION 1 — The nature and extent of sacred doctrine[1]

ARTICLE 1 — Whether, besides philosophy, any further doctrine is required?

On the contrary, It is written (2 Tim. 3:16): "*All Scripture inspired of God is profitable to teach, to reprove, to correct, to instruct in justice.*" Now Scripture, inspired of God, is no part of philosophical science, which has been built up by human reason. Therefore it is useful that besides philosophical science there should be other knowledge—i.e., inspired of God.

I answer that, It was necessary for man's salvation that there should be a knowledge revealed by God, besides philosophical science built up by human reason. Firstly, indeed, because man is directed to God, as to an end that surpasses the grasp of his reason: "*The eye hath not seen, O God, besides Thee, what things Thou hast prepared for them that wait for Thee*" (Isa 66:4). But the end must first be known by men who are to direct thoughts and

---

[1] All quotations from Aquinas, unless otherwise noted, are from *Summa theologica*, trans. Fathers of the English Dominican Province (New York: Benziger Brothers, 1948; reprint, Allen, Texas: Christian Classics, 1981). This translation is available online at, among other places, www.newadvent.org.

actions to the end. Hence it was necessary for the salvation of man that certain truths which exceed human reason should be made known to him by divine revelation. Even as regards those truths about God which human reason could have discovered, it was necessary that man should be taught by a divine revelation; because the truth about God such as reason could discover, would only be known by a few, and that after a long time, and with the admixture of many errors. Whereas man's whole salvation, which is in God, depends upon the knowledge of this truth. Therefore, in order that the salvation of men might be brought about more fitly and more surely, it was necessary that they should be taught divine truths by divine revelation. It was therefore necessary that, besides philosophical science built up by reason, there should be sacred science learned through revelation.

COMMENTARY[2]

Philosophy, a word which means "the love of wisdom," is the search for truth, particularly the truth about God (which is what *wisdom* is, knowledge of the first causes of things), by unaided human reason, that is, unaided by God's revelation. It is called a science in the sense that it is an ordered body of knowledge of the causes (explanations) of things; it is not experimental in the sense in which a science such as chemistry is. But philosophy is not enough for human life, because man has God for his end, the goal of his life. And man needs to know the goal of his life and how to get there if he is to go in the right direction. But man would know neither that God is his goal nor how to reach Him if God had not told him about it in revelation; these are things man cannot know by his own powers. Therefore, since man is made for God, it was necessary for God to reveal Himself as man's end, and there is need of a science, or body of knowledge, beyond philosophy which seeks to understand God's revelation, what today

---

[2] The commentary for this chapter on God owes a great deal to John F. Wippel, *The Metaphysical Thought of Thomas Aquinas* (Washington, D.C.: Catholic University of America Press, 2000).

we call *theology*. We might therefore define theology as "faith seeking understanding," starting from faith, accepting God's revelation, then using human reason to understand it better.

Now, there are some truths about God that can be reached by unaided human reason, by philosophy, namely, that God exists, that there is only one God, and other such attributes of God. But even these are truths that God revealed to man because only a few people have the leisure and mental ability necessary to grasp such proofs without making any errors. Since these truths are necessary for man's salvation, it was fitting for God to reveal them to make them available to all who hear God's word. Those truths that are reachable by human reason but are nevertheless revealed by God are called by Aquinas *preambles of faith*. And, of course, revelation contains many truths that are not reachable by reason, such as the Trinity, Incarnation, and so on, which, according to Aquinas, are *articles of faith*.

I, q. 2, prologue

QUESTION 2 — The existence of God

Prologue. Because the chief aim of sacred doctrine is to teach the knowledge of God, not only as He is in Himself, but also as He is the beginning of things and their last end, and especially of rational creatures, as is clear from what has been already said, therefore, in our endeavor to expound this science, we shall treat: (1) Of God; (2) Of the rational creature's advance towards God; (3) Of Christ, Who as man, is our way to God.

I, q. 2, a. 1

ARTICLE 1 — Whether the existence of God is self-evident?

Objection 2. Further, those things are said to be self-evident which are known as soon as the terms are known, which the Philosopher [Aristotle] (1 Poster. *iii) says is true of the first principles of* demonstration. Thus, when the nature of a whole and of a part is known, it is at once recognized that every whole is greater than its part. But as soon as the signification of the word God is understood, it is at once seen that God exists. For by this word is signified that thing than which nothing greater can be conceived. But that which exists actually and mentally is greater than that which exists only mentally. Therefore, since as soon as the word God is understood it exists mentally, it also follows that it exists actually. Therefore the proposition "God exists" is self-evident.

On the contrary, No one can mentally admit the opposite of what is self-evident; as the Philosopher (Metaph. iv, lec. vi) states concerning the first principles of demonstration. But the opposite of the proposition "God is" can be mentally admitted: "The fool said in his heart, 'There is no God' " (Ps 52:1).[3] Therefore, that God exists is not self-evident.

I answer that, A thing can be self-evident in either of two ways; on the one hand, self-evident in itself, though not to us; on the other, self-evident in itself, and to us. A proposition is self-evident because the predicate is included in the essence of the subject, as "Man is an animal," for animal is contained in the essence of man. If therefore the essence of the predicate and subject be known to all, the proposition will be self-evident to all; as is clear with regard to the first principles of demonstration, the terms of which are common things that no one is ignorant of, such as being and non-being, whole and part, and such like. If, however, there are some to whom the essence of the predicate and subject is unknown, the proposition will be self-evident in itself, but not to those who do not know the meaning of the predicate and subject of the proposition. Therefore, it happens, as Boethius says (Hebdom., the title of which is: "Whether all that is, is good"), "that there are some mental concepts self-evident only to the learned, as that incorporeal substances are not in space." Therefore I say that this

---

[3] This is according to the numbering of the Vulgate. According to the new numbering found in Bibles today, the reference would be to Psalm 53:1. This disparity in numbering applies to most of the Psalms.

proposition, "God exists," of itself is self-evident, for the predicate is the same as the subject; because God is His own existence as will be hereafter shown (q. 3, a. 4). Now because we do not know the essence of God, the proposition is not self-evident to us; but needs to be demonstrated by things that are more known to us, though less known in their nature—namely, by effects.

Reply to Objection 2. *Perhaps not everyone who hears this word* God *understands it to signify something than which nothing greater can be thought, seeing that some have believed God to be a body. Yet, granted that everyone understands that by this word* God *is signified something than which nothing greater can be thought, nevertheless, it does not therefore follow that he understands that what the word signifies exists actually, but only that it exists mentally. Nor can it be argued that it actually exists, unless it be admitted that there actually exists something than which nothing greater can be thought; and this precisely is not admitted by those who hold that God does not exist.*

COMMENTARY

A statement is self-evidently true if it is seen to be true once its terms are understood. More precisely, a statement is self-evident if the predicate is part of the essence of the subject. Aquinas gives the example of "Man is an animal." If man is defined as a *rational animal*, then "animal" is part of the essence of man, the *essence* being *what* something is. Other examples of self-evident truths include the principle of non-contradiction, "A thing cannot both be and not-be at the same time and in the same respect," and "a whole is greater than its part."

Now, Aquinas makes a distinction between (1) propositions (statements) that are self-evident in themselves and self-evident to us and (2) propositions that are self-evident in themselves but not self-evident to us. He claims that "God exists" is self-evident in itself because the predicate, existence, is contained in the essence of the subject, God. Aquinas is saying that existence is part of, or is, God's essence, that essence and existence are identical in God, that God is

Existence Itself. This sets God apart from every other being because in every other being essence and existence are really distinct (not identical), such that existence is caused in those things by something else (ultimately, God). But this is not known to us apart from a philosophical proof or demonstration because we do not know the essence of God in this life. If we did, we would see that His essence is existence. In this life, though, lacking that knowledge of God's essence, to know that God exists requires a demonstration.

Objection 2 presents reasoning that is close to that of St. Anselm. Anselm's argument for God's existence, which Aquinas here understands to be tantamount to the claim that God's existence is self-evident, is known as the Ontological Argument. The claim of the argument is that God's existence is known once the word *God* is understood to mean "that than which nothing greater can be thought." If something is thought than which a greater cannot be thought, it must exist in reality, for if it existed only in the mind, it would not be the greatest conceivable thing, since it is obviously greater to exist both in the mind and in reality than merely in the mind alone. But Aquinas rejects this way of thinking because it improperly moves from the realm of thought to reality. One cannot conclude that the greatest conceivable thing exists in reality simply because one thinks it in the mind. All that the argument will yield is a greatest conceivable thing existing in the mind, but not necessarily in (extra-mental) reality. Some other sort of proof is needed for that conclusion, namely, one that starts from some feature of the created world and moves toward its cause, God.

I, q. 2, a. 2

ARTICLE 2 — **Whether it can be demonstrated that God exists?**

> *Objection 1. It seems that the existence of God cannot be demonstrated. For it is an article of faith that God exists. But what is of faith cannot be demonstrated, because a demonstration produces scientific knowledge; whereas faith is of the unseen (Heb 11:1). Therefore it cannot be demonstrated that God exists.*

On the contrary, *The Apostle says: "The invisible things of Him are clearly seen, being understood by the things that are made" (Rom 1:20). But this would not be unless the existence of God could be demonstrated through the things that are made; for the first thing we must know of anything is, whether it exists.*

I answer that, *Demonstration can be made in two ways: One is through the cause, and is called* a priori, *and this is to argue from what is prior absolutely. The other is through the effect, and is called a demonstration* a posteriori; *this is to argue from what is prior relatively only to us. When an effect is better known to us than its cause, from the effect we proceed to the knowledge of the cause. And from every effect the existence of its proper cause can be demonstrated, so long as its effects are better known to us; because since every effect depends upon its cause, if the effect exists, the cause must pre-exist. Hence the existence of God, in so far as it is not self-evident to us, can be demonstrated from those of His effects which are known to us.*

Reply to Objection 1. *The existence of God and other like truths about God, which can be known by natural reason, are not articles of faith, but preambles to the articles; for faith presupposes natural knowledge, even as grace presupposes nature, and perfection supposes something that can be perfected. Nevertheless, there is nothing to prevent a man, who cannot grasp a proof, accepting, as a matter of faith, something which in itself is capable of being scientifically known and demonstrated.*[4]

COMMENTARY

Aquinas speaks of two kinds of philosophical demonstration:[5] (1) *propter quid*, or reasoning from cause to effect (which is done, for example, in geometry); (2) *quia*, or reasoning from effect to cause. He

---

[4] Not according to an experimental science, but according to philosophical knowledge.

[5] Now for a short course in logic: A philosophical demonstration is a deductive argument (a syllogism) that produces certain and necessary (cannot be other

singles out the latter as the kind of demonstration capable of showing that God exists. After all, we have to start with what we know, or what is better known to us. And the world around us is certainly better known to us than anything that might transcend, or exist beyond, the world. So perhaps we can examine the world, some features of the world, or its very existence to see if it points to the existence of a cause outside of itself that makes it to be. The existence of an effect implies the existence, or "pre-existence," of its cause.

The Scripture text in the "On the contrary" section, from Romans 1:20, is the text that the Church cites to show that proving God's existence philosophically can be done. In fact, Vatican I taught that God's existence can be proved in philosophy, so this is something to which Catholics must assent. It does not mean that each person must be able to furnish or follow such a proof, but only that it is possible for human reason to discover one.

In fact, in the reply to objection 1, Aquinas refers again to the preambles of faith, truths which can be proved philosophically but are also revealed by God for those who cannot grasp such a proof. Nothing prevents those who cannot grasp a proof of God from accepting His existence as a matter of faith. But it would not be possible for one and the same person to both know that God exists through a demonstration and accept His existence through faith; those two states exclude each other in such a way that they cannot exist simultaneously in a single person.

It should be noted that Aquinas here also refers to a well-known axiom of his, namely, that faith builds upon, and does not destroy, natural knowledge, just as grace builds upon, and does not destroy, nature.

---

wise) knowledge (*scientia* in Latin, which at its best tells us why things are as they are, the causes of things). A *valid* syllogism is one in which premises entail or demand the conclusion; if the premises are true, then the conclusion must be true as well. And a valid syllogism with true premises is called *sound*. And if a sound argument has certain and necessary premises, producing a certain and necessary conclusion, then it is a demonstration. A simple example would be:

All men are mortal.	(Premise)
Socrates is a man.	(Premise)
Socrates is mortal.	(Conclusion)

Chapter One — God

Aquinas does not see faith as being at odds with natural knowledge; both have their ultimate source in God and therefore cannot contradict each other, since God cannot deceive nor contradict Himself.

I, q. 2, a. 3
Article 3 — Whether God exists?

Objection 1. *It seems that God does not exist; because if one of two contraries be infinite, the other would be altogether destroyed. But the word* God *means that He is infinite goodness. If, therefore, God existed, there would be no evil discoverable; but there is evil in the world. Therefore God does not exist.*

On the contrary*, It is said in the person of God: "I am Who am" (Exod 3:14).*

I answer that*, The existence of God can be proved in five ways.*

The first and more manifest way is the argument from motion. It is certain, and evident to our senses, that in the world some things are in motion. Now whatever is in motion is put in motion by another, for nothing can be in motion except it is in potentiality to that towards which it is in motion; whereas a thing moves inasmuch as it is in act. For motion is nothing else than the reduction of something from potentiality to actuality. But nothing can be reduced from potentiality to actuality, except by something in a state of actuality. Thus that which is actually hot, as fire, makes wood, which is potentially hot, to be actually hot, and thereby moves and changes it. Now it is not possible that the same thing should be at once in actuality and potentiality in the same respect, but only in different respects. For what is actually hot cannot simultaneously be potentially hot; but it is simultaneously potentially cold. It is therefore impossible that in the same respect and in the same way a thing should be both mover and moved, i.e., that it should move itself. Therefore, whatever is in motion must be put in motion by another. If that by which it is put in motion be itself put in motion, then this also must needs be put in motion by another, and that by another again. But this cannot go on to infinity, because then there would be no first mover, and, consequently, no other mover; seeing that subsequent movers move only inasmuch as they are put in motion by the first mover; as the staff moves only because it is put in motion by the hand. Therefore it is necessary to arrive at a first mover, put in motion by no other; and this everyone understands to be God.

The second way is from the nature of the efficient cause. In the world of sense we find there is an order of efficient causes. There is no case known (neither is it, indeed, possible) in which a thing is found to be the efficient cause of itself; for so it would be prior to itself, which is impossible. Now in efficient causes it is not possible to go on to infinity, because in all efficient causes following in order, the first is the cause of the intermediate cause, and the intermediate cause is the cause of the ultimate cause, whether the intermediate cause be several, or one only. Now to take away the cause is to take away the effect. Therefore, if there be no first cause among the efficient causes, there will be no ultimate, nor any intermediate cause. But if in efficient causes it is possible to go on to infinity, there will be no first efficient cause, neither will there be an ultimate effect, nor any intermediate efficient causes; all of which is plainly false. Therefore it is necessary to admit a first efficient cause, to which everyone gives the name of God.

The third way is taken from possibility and necessity, and runs thus. We find in nature things that are possible to be and not to be, since they are found to be generated, and to corrupt, and consequently, they are possible to be and not to be. But it is impossible for these always to exist, for that which is possible not to be at some time is not. Therefore, if everything is possible not to be, then at one time there could have been nothing in existence. Now if this were true, even now there would be nothing in existence, because that which does not exist only begins to exist by something already existing. Therefore, if at one time nothing was in existence, it would have been impossible for anything to have begun to exist; and thus even now nothing would be in existence—

which is absurd. Therefore, not all beings are merely possible, but there must exist something the existence of which is necessary. But every necessary thing either has its necessity caused by another, or not. Now it is impossible to go on to infinity in necessary things which have their necessity caused by another, as has been already proved in regard to efficient causes. Therefore we cannot but postulate the existence of some being having of itself its own necessity, and not receiving it from another, but rather causing in others their necessity. This all men speak of as God.

The fourth way is taken from the gradation to be found in things. Among beings there are some more and some less good, true, noble, and the like. But "more" and "less" are predicated of different things, according as they resemble in their different ways something which is the maximum, as a thing is said to be hotter according as it more nearly resembles that which is hottest; so that there is something which is truest, something best, something noblest, and, consequently, something which is uttermost being; for those things that are greatest in truth are greatest in being, as it is written in Metaph. *ii. Now the maximum in any genus is the cause of all in that genus; as fire, which is the maximum of heat, is the cause of all hot things. Therefore there must also be something which is to all beings the cause of their being, goodness, and every other perfection; and this we call God.*

The fifth way is taken from the governance of the world. We see that things which lack intelligence, such as natural bodies, act for an end, and this is evident from their acting always, or nearly always, in the same way, so as to obtain the best result. Hence it is plain that not fortuitously, but designedly, do they achieve their end. Now whatever lacks intelligence cannot move towards an end, unless it be directed by some being endowed with knowledge and intelligence; as the arrow is shot to its mark by the archer. Therefore some intelligent being exists by whom all natural things are directed to their end; and this being we call God.

Reply to Objection 1. *As Augustine says (*Enchir. *xi): "Since God is the highest good, He would not allow any evil to exist in*

His works, unless His omnipotence and goodness were such as to bring good even out of evil." This is part of the infinite goodness of God, that He should allow evil to exist, and out of it produce good.

Commentary

This article presents Aquinas's famous Five Ways, five arguments for God's existence. Actually, what is concluded to in each case is (1) a first mover, (2) a first cause, (3) necessary being, (4) a maximally great being, and (5) an intelligent director of the universe. These descriptions may not seem divine enough to satisfy us that God's existence has really been proved. But Aquinas will go on to draw many other conclusions about the first being from these five starting points. So, the description of God, His attributes, will begin to fill out as Aquinas continues to argue.

Note on Infinite Regresses

In the first three of the five ways, Aquinas denies an infinite regress of, respectively, moved movers, efficient causes, and necessary beings whose necessity is caused. Now, there are two types of infinite regress. One is historical and the other simultaneous. Aquinas is not concerned to deny the possibility of a historical infinite regress, one that stretches back in time. An example of this type of regress is a father begetting a son, who in turn begets a son, who in turn begets a son, and so on. If we pick the most recent effect, a son, and look back at the series that produced him, Aquinas thinks there is no reason to deny that such a series may extend back infinitely. This is true in part because he thinks that a universe that always existed cannot be disproved philosophically (though he believes by faith that the universe was created a finite time ago), an issue that will be discussed later.

But an infinite regress where the causes are acting simultaneously and not stretching back in time is more problematic. Consider the case where a bucket in a well is pulled up by a rope, which in turn is pulled by a pulley, which is operated by a crank, which is turned by the arm and hand of a farmer. The ultimate effect, the raising of the bucket, is brought about by a series of causes (the rope and pulley), which are themselves effects of other causes. This type of series cannot be infinite, but only in a sense. The sense in which it cannot be infinite is if a first, uncaused cause is denied. If there is no first, uncaused cause of whatever effect is being looked at, then there will be no intermediate causes and effects, and no ultimate effect either. It does not matter how many intermediate causes and effects there are, infinite or finite, there must be a first, uncaused cause, or else there will no intermediates and no final effect. That's the sense in which Aquinas denies the possibility of an infinite series or regress of causes and effects.

An example of an absurd infinite regress might be this: I ask to borrow a book from Joe, but Joe has to borrow it from Fred, but Fred has to borrow it from Bill, but Bill has to borrow it from Jack, and so on. If that sort of series is infinite, then I will never get the book, because everyone has to borrow it, but no one actually *has* or *possesses* the book.[6] Someone must *have* the book if I'm ever going to receive it. In the same way, if an effect that we try to account for (say, motion or contingent existence) has no first, uncaused cause, a thing that uniquely *has* the effect (for example, existence) or the unique power to cause the effect (for example, motion), then there will be no final effect to account for.

First Way

The First Way starts from motion, but not only local motion, or motion from place to place is in mind here. There are other kinds of motion: increase/decrease in size, qualitative motion (for example, going from cold to hot), and generation/corruption of an individual (which is actually thought of by Aquinas as, technically speaking, a change rather than a motion). It might be better, therefore, to think of the First Way as dealing with the wider notion of change, a notion wide enough to cover the types of motion (and change) mentioned above. Really, Aquinas is thinking of any reduction from potency to act, that is, any "movement" from what can be the case to what is the case. *Potency* and *act* are easy enough to understand: I do not have red

---

[6] This argument is drawn from Peter Kreeft and Ronald K. Tacelli, *Handbook of Christian Apologetics* (Downers Grove, IL: InterVarsity Press, 1994), 51.

hair but I could have red hair if I dyed it. I have the potential for red hair; it is something that can be. Now if I go ahead and dye it, I'll actually have red hair; at that point, it is something that is. I will go from potentially having red hair to actually having it. And this sort of change or motion requires an outside cause. My hair cannot change itself from brown to red; an outside agent must act on it, namely, a dye. This is why Aquinas says that whatever is moved is moved by another. A thing cannot reduce, or "move," itself from potency to act; some other cause must bring about the motion or change. Since there cannot be an infinite regress of moved movers, one must arrive at an unmoved mover, the unmoved source of all motion and change in the world. If this first, unmoved mover did not exist, there would be no motion or change in the world, which is obviously absurd. Therefore, such an unmoved mover must exist.

Finally, we can see that this unmoved source of all movement and change must be pure act with no potency for change. So, not only is this being unmoved but also immovable; it cannot be moved because it has no potency for movement or change, and besides, no higher being than it to actualize any potency one might suppose it to have.

Second Way

This argument focuses on the efficient cause of motion or change. The background to this is Aristotle's doctrine of the four causes: efficient, formal, material, and final. Think of sculpting a statue out of marble. The sculptor is the efficient cause, the marble is the material cause, the shape of the statue is the formal cause, and the completion of the statue is the final cause, or the goal which the efficient cause (the sculptor) has in mind. So the efficient cause is what brings about motion or change, or brings about a beginning or continuation in existence; in the above example, the efficient cause is the one who actualizes the potency of the matter (marble) to become a statue. The Second Way is focusing on a series of efficient causes that cannot be infinite; there must be a first, uncaused cause, or else there would not be a last efficient cause or a final effect of that cause, which is absurd. Therefore, there must exist an uncaused cause that brings about all of the efficient causes and their effects within the universe, the source of all efficient causality.

Third Way

This way begins from the notions of possible (or contingent) being and necessary being. *Possible* being is being that need not be, being that can not-be. *Necessary* being is being that must be, that cannot not-be. When Aquinas speaks of necessary beings that have their necessity caused, he has in mind immaterial beings, such as angels (and perhaps other heavenly bodies that cannot corrupt because, though material, their form so fulfills the potency of their matter as to leave no further potency to corrupt). Because immaterial beings have no matter, they have no potency to corrupt. Since they have no potency or tendency to corrupt within their own natures, these beings have a kind of necessity; once they exist, they will not cease to exist (unless God annihilates them, which we trust He will not do). These beings have, therefore, a necessity that is caused, a necessity caused by an absolutely necessary being, God, Whose very nature is existence. Only God's necessity is uncaused.

Many commentators believe that the way Aquinas has stated the Third Way involves him in a logical fallacy, which would make the Third Way an invalid argument. The problematic move occurs when Aquinas introduces a temporal or historical element to the argument. He claims, "If everything can not-be, then at one time there was nothing in existence." From there, of course, it makes sense to conclude that since there are obviously things in existence now, it must not be the case that at one time everything passed out of existence, because from nothing comes nothing. But the questionable premise appears to commit the Fallacy of Composition. This logical fallacy is an illegal move from the character of the parts of a whole to a claim about the character of the whole. If one said that because each brick in this pile weighs two pounds, then the whole pile of bricks weighs two pounds, that person would be committing the composition fallacy. Here in the Third Way, Aquinas seems to do the same thing, moving from the (supposed) possible nature of each thing[7] to the claim that every

---

[7] He supposes every being is a possible being for the sake of argument, in an effort to show that this results in absurd consequences, a form of reasoning known as a *reduction to the absurd*.

being taken together as a whole or a group is possible or contingent and therefore would have, at some time in an infinite past, passed out of existence. So he seems to rely on fallacious reasoning to reach the supposition of every possible or contingent being passing out of existence at one and the same time so that nothing would at that time, and from then on, exist (which is clearly counter-factual since things do exist now). This form of reasoning ignores the possibility that there could have been a series of contingent beings such that each one eventually passed out of existence, but not all of them at the same time; one might pass away, but it might produce another one before passing away, which could produce another before it too passed away, and so on. In other texts (namely, *Summa contra Gentiles* I.15[8] and II.15) Aquinas has stated this argument without the troublesome historical or temporal feature, which makes for a better, non-fallacious argument. In those places, he simply focuses on the need for an absolutely necessary being, God, to cause the contingent beings with which we are acquainted—no First Cause of being, no effect. But we know the effect exists, so we know that the cause must exist as well.

Fourth Way

This argument is the least favorite of most commentators on Aquinas as it seems to be the weakest. We must admit, however, that it has a kind of intuitive appeal, since the gradations among things (some things are greater than others, more beautiful, and so on) do seem to

---

[8] For instance: "We find in the world, furthermore, certain beings, those namely that are subject to generation and corruption, which can be and not-be. But what can be has a cause because, since it is equally related to two contraries, namely, being and not-being, it must be owing to some cause that being accrues to it. Now, as we have proved by the reasoning of Aristotle, one cannot proceed to infinity among causes. We must therefore posit something that is a necessary being. Every necessary being, however, either has the cause of its necessity in an outside source or, if it does not, it is necessary through itself. But one cannot proceed to infinity among necessary beings the cause of whose necessity lies in an outside source. We must therefore posit a first necessary being, which is necessary through itself. This is God, since, as we have shown, He is the first cause." *Summa contra Gentiles*, Book One: *God*, trans. Anton Pegis (Notre Dame: University of Notre Dame Press, 1975), chapter 15.

imply an absolute standard. Notice also that Aquinas still introduces the Maximal or Greatest Being as being the cause of all the other, lesser beings for which it serves as the standard of perfection. So even in this attempted proof, Aquinas does not leave behind the perspective of looking for God as the cause of the world, in this case, the cause of the varying perfection of things.

Fifth Way

The Fifth Way is an argument based on the end-directedness or goal-directedness found in nature. If you look at the development of an animal, say, a horse, both within its mother's womb and once it is born, we see that a healthy adult horse comes to be always or for the most part. The natural process of development ends up with what is good for the horse, fully developed, healthy adulthood. That is what is good for the horse and what is in some sense "sought" within the process. Such a "purposeful" process cannot be the result of chance, because what happens by chance is necessarily or by definition rare, not something that happens always or for the most part. Yet this end-directedness within nature requires intelligence to do the directing. Therefore the natural process of horse development is directed by an outside intelligence toward its goal. Now, all of nature exhibits this end-directedness, so all of nature is directed by an intelligent being.

Reply to Objection 1

This is the classic answer to the problem of evil. If God is all-good and all-powerful, then how can there be evil in the world, either moral evil or physical evil? Well, moral evil is traceable to the free actions of human beings (and angels). But the deepest reason that the reality of evil is not incompatible with the existence of the Christian God is that God has fought and is fighting and overcoming evil, most especially in His Son, Jesus Christ. So, God would allow no evil in His creation except what He can and will turn to an even greater good. The prime example is the sin of Adam and Eve, the "happy fault, which won for us so great a Redeemer" (Easter Exsultet).

I, q. 3, a. 4

QUESTION 3 — **Of the simplicity of God**

ARTICLE 4 — **Whether essence and existence are the same in God?**

I answer that, God is not only His own essence, as shown in the preceding article, but also His own existence. This may be shown in several ways. First, whatever a thing has besides its essence must be caused either by the constituent principles of that essence (like a property that necessarily accompanies the species—as the faculty of laughing is proper to a man—and is caused by the constituent principles of the species), or by some exterior agent,—as heat is caused in water by fire. Therefore, if the existence of a thing differs from its essence, this existence must be caused either by some exterior agent or by its essential principles. Now it is impossible for a thing's existence to be caused by its essential constituent principles, for nothing can be the sufficient cause of its own existence, if its existence is caused. Therefore that thing, whose existence differs from its essence, must have its existence caused by another. But this cannot be true of God; because we call God the first efficient cause. Therefore it is impossible that in God His existence should differ from His essence. . . .

COMMENTARY

Here we have Aquinas specifically dealing with the issue of God's essence and existence being identical. The nub of the argument is that in every being other than God, essence and existence are really distinct, and the reason they each have existence (do exist) is that something causes existence to come to them (God). God, however, is the First Being and First Cause, so existence cannot come to Him from a higher cause or agent. Therefore, essence and existence are identical in God; it is His very nature (which means basically the same thing as "essence") to exist.

I, q. 13, a. 2

QUESTION 13 — The names of God

ARTICLE 2 — Whether any name can be applied to God substantially?

Objection 3. Further, a thing is named by us according as we understand it. But God is not understood by us in this life in His substance. Therefore neither is any name we can use applied substantially to God.

I answer that, Negative names applied to God or signifying His relation to creatures manifestly do not at all signify His substance, but rather express the distance of the creature from Him, or His relation to something else, or rather, the relation of creatures to Himself.

But as regards absolute and affirmative names of God, as good, wise, and the like, various and many opinions have been given. For some have said that all such names, although they are applied to God affirmatively, nevertheless have been brought into use more to express some remotion from God, rather than to express anything that exists positively in Him. Hence they assert that when we say that God lives, we mean that God is not like an inanimate thing; and the same in like manner applies to other names; and this was taught by Rabbi Moses. Others say that these names applied to God signify His relationship towards creatures: thus in the words, "God is good," we mean, "God is the cause of goodness in things"; and the same rule applies to other names.

Both of these opinions, however, seem to be untrue for three reasons. First because in neither of them can a reason be assigned why some names more than others are applied to God. For He is assuredly the cause of bodies in the same way as He is the cause of good things; therefore if the words "God is good," signified no more than, "God is the cause of good things," it might in like manner be said that God is a body, inasmuch as He is the cause of bodies. So also to say that He is a body implies that He is not a mere potentiality, as is primary matter. Secondly, because it would follow that all names applied to God would be said of Him by way of being taken in a secondary sense, as healthy is secondarily said of medicine, forasmuch as it signifies only the cause of health in the animal which primarily is called healthy. Thirdly, because this is against the intention of those who speak of God. For in saying that God lives, they assuredly mean more than to say that He is the cause of our life, or that He differs from inanimate bodies.

Therefore we must hold a different doctrine—viz., that these names signify the divine substance, and are predicated substantially of God, although they fall short of a full representation of Him. Which is proved thus. For these names express God, so far as our intellects know Him. Now since our intellect knows God from creatures, it knows Him as far as creatures represent Him. Now it was shown above (q. 4, a. 2) that God prepossesses in Himself all the perfections of creatures, being Himself simply and universally perfect. Hence every creature represents Him, and is like Him so far as it possesses some perfection: yet it represents Him not as something of the same species or genus, but as the excelling principle of whose form the effects fall short, although they derive some kind of likeness thereto, even as the forms of inferior bodies represent the power of the sun. This was explained above (q. 4, a. 3), in treating of the divine perfection. Therefore the aforesaid names signify the divine substance, but in an imperfect manner, even as creatures represent it imperfectly. So when we say, "God is good," the meaning is not, "God is the cause of goodness," or, "God is not evil"; but the meaning is, "Whatever good we attribute to creatures, pre-exists in God," and in a more excellent and higher way. Hence it does not follow that God is good, because He causes goodness; but rather, on the contrary, He causes goodness in things because He is good; according to what Augustine says (De Doctr. Christ. i.32), "Because He is good, we are."

Reply to Objection 3. *We cannot know the essence of God in this life, as He really is in Himself; but we know Him accord-*

ingly as He is represented in the perfections of creatures; and thus the names imposed by us signify Him in that manner only.

I, q. 13, a. 5

ARTICLE 5 — **Whether what is said of God and of creatures is univocally predicated of them?**

I answer that, Univocal predication is impossible between God and creatures. The reason of this is that every effect which is not an adequate result of the power of the efficient cause, receives the similitude of the agent not in its full degree, but in a measure that falls short, so that what is divided and multiplied in the effects resides in the agent simply, and in the same manner; as for example the sun by the exercise of its one power produces manifold and various forms in all inferior things. In the same way, as said in the preceding article, all perfections existing in creatures divided and multiplied, pre-exist in God unitedly. Thus, when any term expressing perfection is applied to a creature, it signifies that perfection distinct in idea from other perfections; as, for instance, by this term *wise* applied to a man, we signify some perfection distinct from a man's essence, and distinct from his power and existence, and from all similar things; whereas when we apply it to God, we do not mean to signify anything distinct from His essence, or power, or existence. Thus also this term *wise* applied to man in some degree circumscribes and comprehends the thing signified; whereas this is not the case when it is applied to God; but it leaves the thing signified as incomprehended, and as exceeding the signification of the name. Hence it is evident that this term *wise* is not applied in the same way to God and to man. The same rule applies to other terms. Hence no name is predicated univocally of God and of creatures.

Neither, on the other hand, are names applied to God and creatures in a purely equivocal sense, as some have said. Because if that were so, it follows that from creatures nothing could be *known or demonstrated about God at all; for the reasoning would always be exposed to the fallacy of equivocation. Such a view is against the philosophers, who proved many things about God, and also against what the Apostle says: "The invisible things of God are clearly seen being understood by the things that are made" (Rom 1:20). Therefore it must be said that these names are said of God and creatures in an analogous sense, that is, according to proportion.*

Now names are thus used in two ways: either according as many things are proportionate to one, thus for example healthy *is predicated of medicine and urine in relation and in proportion to health of a body, of which the latter is the sign and the former the cause: or according as one thing is proportionate to another, thus* healthy *is said of medicine and animal, since medicine is the cause of health in the animal body. And in this way some things are said of God and creatures analogically, and not in a purely equivocal nor in a purely univocal sense. For we can name God only from creatures (a. 1). Thus, whatever is said of God and creatures, is said according to the relation of a creature to God as its principle and cause, wherein all perfections of things pre-exist excellently. Now this mode of community of idea is a mean between pure equivocation and simple univocation. For in analogies the idea is not, as it is in univocals, one and the same, yet it is not totally diverse as in equivocals; but a term which is thus used in a multiple sense signifies various proportions to some one thing; thus* healthy *applied to urine signifies the sign of animal health, and applied to medicine signifies the cause of the same health.*

COMMENTARY

In these two articles, Aquinas is concerned to understand how we can speak about God, Who is infinitely superior to His creatures. We can break down speech about God into two types: positive and negative. To speak negatively of God means to deny certain things of God. For instance, we might say: "God is not material" or "God is not limited." In such a case, we are saying what God is not; we are removing limitations and imperfections from our speech about God in order to speak truly of Him. But this obviously yields no positive knowledge of God, only negative knowledge.

So what about positive speech about God? For instance, "God is good," "God is wise," and so on? Is this acceptable, and, if so, how does it work? We draw our concepts and our words from our experience of creatures. If we try to apply such words to God, does it mean the same thing when applied to God as it does when applied to creatures? The three choices for positive speech about God are the following: univocal predication, equivocal predication, and analogical predication. *Univocal* predication involves using the same word with the same concept (intelligible content). An example of this is "John threw the *ball* to the pitcher" and "The pitcher caught the *ball*." The word *ball* is used univocally in this instance. *Equivocal* predication involves using the same word with a completely different concept (intelligible content). An example would be "John swung the *bat* at the ball" and "The *bat* flew out of the cave." *Analogical* predication involves the same word but with a concept (intelligible content) that is partly the same and partly different. An example would be: "That broccoli is *healthy*" and "According to the thermometer, his temperature is *healthy*." In the first sentence, healthy is predicated of broccoli because it is a cause of health in a human being. In the second sentence, healthy is predicated of the temperature because a good temperature is a sign of health in a human being. In each case, *healthy* means something a little different, but each use is united by being related to one proper subject of health, the healthy human being or animal.

Analogical predication is the kind of predication or speech that applies to talking about God. We draw our words from creatures but in the case of words such as *good* or *wise* (pure perfections, which imply no intrinsic limitation or imperfection) the words belong most properly to God. The reason is that He is supremely good and wise and grants us a limited share in wisdom and goodness by creating us. Now, the goodness and wisdom of creatures is not wholly different from God's goodness and wisdom because every effect is like its cause (so, partly the same). But the goodness and wisdom of creatures is not wholly the same as God's because God possesses those perfections in an infinite and unlimited (super-eminent) way, whereas creatures have them in a limited and finite way (so, partly different). Analogical predication is the way, then, that we can speak in a positive fashion about God and have positive knowledge of Him.

I, q. 46, a. 2

QUESTION 46 — Of the beginning of the duration of creatures

ARTICLE 2 — Whether it is an article of faith that the world began?

Objection 1. *It would seem that it is not an article of faith but a demonstrable conclusion that the world began. For everything that is made has a beginning of its duration. But it can be proved demonstratively that God is the effective cause of the world; indeed this is asserted by the more approved philosophers. Therefore it can be demonstratively proved that the world began.*

On the contrary, *The articles of faith cannot be proved demonstratively, because faith is of things "that appear not" (Heb 11:1). But that God is the Creator of the world: hence that the world began, is an article of faith; for we say, "I believe in one God," etc. And again, Gregory says (*Hom. i. in Ezech.*), that Moses prophesied of the past, saying, "In the beginning God created heaven and earth," in which words the newness of the world is stated. Therefore the newness of the world is known only by revelation; and therefore it cannot be proved demonstratively.*

I answer that, *By faith alone do we hold, and by no demonstration can it be proved, that the world did not always exist, as was said above of the mystery of the Trinity (q. 32, a.1). The reason of this is that the newness of the world cannot be demonstrated on the part of the world itself. For the principle of demonstration is the essence of a thing. Now everything accord-*

ing to its species is abstracted from here *and* now; *whence it is said that universals are everywhere and always. Hence it cannot be demonstrated that man, or heaven, or a stone were not always. Likewise neither can it be demonstrated on the part of the efficient cause, which acts by will. For the will of God cannot be investigated by reason, except as regards those things which God must will of necessity; and what He wills about creatures is not among these, as was said above (q. 19, a. 3). But the divine will can be manifested by revelation, on which faith rests. Hence that the world began to exist is an object of faith, but not of demonstration or science. And it is useful to consider this, lest anyone, presuming to demonstrate what is of faith, should bring forward reasons that are not cogent, so as to give occasion to unbelievers to laugh, thinking that on such grounds we believe things that are of faith.*

Reply to Objection 1. *As Augustine says (* De Civ. Dei *xi.4), the opinion of philosophers who asserted the eternity of the world was twofold. For some said that the substance of the world was not from God, which is an intolerable error; and therefore it is refuted by proofs that are cogent. Some, however, said that the world is eternal, although made by God. For they hold that the world has a beginning, not of time, but of creation, so that in a certain hardly intelligible way it was always made. And they try to explain their meaning thus (* De Civ. Dei *x.31): "for as, if the foot were always in the dust from eternity, there would always be a footprint which without doubt was caused by him who trod on it, so also the world always was, because its Maker always existed." To understand this we must consider that the efficient cause, which acts by motion, of necessity precedes its effect in time; because the effect is only in the end of the action, and every agent must be the principle of action. But if the action is instantaneous and not successive, it is not necessary for the maker to be prior to the thing made in duration, as appears in the case of illumination. Hence they say that it does not follow necessarily if God is the active cause of the world, that He should be prior to the world* *in duration; because creation, by which He produced the world, is not a successive change, as was said above (q. 45, a. 2).*

COMMENTARY

For Aquinas, that the world is only a finite age, that it began some finite time ago, is an article of faith, and cannot be proved by a philosophical demonstration. He seems to think, though it may not be clear in this article, that God could have created a universe with no temporal beginning, one that was infinitely old. Such a universe would still be created by and dependent upon God, but it would have depended on God infinitely into the past. Such a possibility would not make the universe eternal, strictly speaking. God alone is strictly *eternal*, which means outside of time or timeless, beyond the change and succession that time measures. But Christians such as Aquinas believe by faith that the world began a finite time ago because that's what the Bible teaches in Genesis. It's just something that cannot be proved by reason alone.

CHAPTER TWO

MAN

I, q. 75, a. 1

QUESTION 75 — **Of man who is composed of a spiritual and a corporeal substance: And in the first place, concerning what belongs to the essence of the soul**

ARTICLE 1 — **Whether the soul is a body?**

On the contrary, Augustine says (De Trin. vi.6) that the soul "is simple in comparison with the body, inasmuch as it does not occupy space by its bulk."

I answer that, To seek the nature of the soul, we must premise that the soul is defined as the first principle of life in those things which live: for we call living things *animate, and those things which have no life,* inanimate. *Now life is shown principally by two actions, knowledge and movement. The philosophers of old, not being able to rise above their imagination, supposed that the principle of these actions was something corporeal: for they asserted that only bodies were real things; and that what is not corporeal is nothing: hence they maintained that the soul is something corporeal. This opinion can be proved to be false in many ways; but we shall make use of only one proof, based on universal and certain principles, which shows clearly that the soul is not a body.*

It is manifest that not every principle of vital action is a soul, for then the eye would be a soul, as it is a principle of vision; and the same might be applied to the other instruments of the soul: but it is the first *principle of life, which we call the soul. Now, though a body may be a principle of life, as the heart is a principle of life in an animal, yet nothing corporeal can be the first principle of life. For it is clear that to be a principle of life, or to be a living thing, does not belong to a body as such; since, if that were the case, every body would be a living thing, or a principle of life. Therefore a body is competent to be a living thing or even a principle of life, as* such *a body. Now that it is actually such a body, it owes to some principle which is called its act. Therefore the soul, which is the first principle of life, is not a body, but the act of a body; thus heat, which is the principle of calefaction, is not a body, but an act of a body.*

Commentary

Here, we get some sort of definition or description of the *soul*, namely, the first principle or source of life in a living thing. This means that anything that shares in life has some sort of soul, including humans, non-human animals, and even plants. But two activities that especially manifest the presence of life, knowledge and movement, seem to place souls most properly in animals and humans. And we also come to understand here that the soul and the body go together as substantial form to matter, as act to potency. A *substantial form* is the intrinsic principle or source within a thing which makes it to be *what* it is, makes it be the kind of thing it is, for example, a dog, a horse, a human being. The soul informs the potency and makes the body be a living body of a certain kind; it is the actualizing principle of the body. So, the soul and body of any living thing form a close union.

I, q. 75, a. 2

ARTICLE 2 — Whether the human soul is something subsistent?

I answer that, It must necessarily be allowed that the principle of intellectual operation which we call the soul, is a principle both incorporeal and subsistent. For it is clear that by means of the intellect man can have knowledge of all corporeal things. Now whatever knows certain things cannot have any of them in its own nature; because that which is in it naturally would impede the knowledge of anything else. Thus we observe that a sick man's tongue being vitiated by a feverish and bitter humor, is insensible to anything sweet, and everything seems bitter to it. Therefore, if the intellectual principle contained the nature of a body it would be unable to know all bodies. Now every body has its own determinate nature. Therefore it is impossible for the intellectual principle to be a body. It is likewise impossible for it to understand by means of a bodily organ; since the determinate nature of that organ would impede knowledge of all bodies; as when a certain determinate color is not only in the pupil of the eye, but also in a glass vase, the liquid in the vase seems to be of that same color.

Therefore the intellectual principle which we call the mind or the intellect has an operation per se *apart from the body. Now only that which subsists can have an operation* per se. *For nothing can operate but what is actual: wherefore a thing operates according as it is; for which reason we do not say that heat imparts heat, but that what is hot gives heat. We must conclude, therefore, that the human soul, which is called the intellect or the mind, is something incorporeal and subsistent.*

COMMENTARY

This article bears on the question of the immortality of the human soul, whether the soul can survive human death and go on existing. If the human soul is *subsistent*, this means that it is in some way a substance existing in its own right, an independently existing thing (though always dependent upon God) that can go on existing without the body. Animal souls certainly cannot survive the death of the individual since those souls are not subsistent; such souls depend for their existence on the body, just as their bodies depend on their souls. When death comes to animals, the soul goes out of existence, and the body is no longer alive and begins to decay. But if the human soul is subsistent, then the story might be different.

Aquinas goes about showing that the human soul is subsistent by showing that it has an operation—intellection or understanding—that is independent of the body. Operation follows being or displays being, so if the human soul *operates* independently of the body, then the human soul *exists* or *can exist* independently of the body.

Therefore, it remains only to show that the human intellect or mind can operate independently of the body. Aquinas argues that because it can understand all bodies, can understand the natures of all bodies, it must not be a body. If the intellect were a body, or had the nature of a body, having that determinate nature would impede its ability to understand all bodily things; its capacity to know would be restricted in scope by its bodiliness. To put it another way, if the intellect intrinsically depended upon a bodily organ, the determinate bodily nature of that organ would impede the intellect's ability to understand all forms; it would wreck its universal openness and receptivity. Therefore, the intellect operates independently of the body and so the human soul can exist independently of the body, is incorporeal (non-bodily) and subsistent.

It is true, however, that the intellect does have a kind of dependence on the body, namely, an extrinsic dependence on bodily organs. For it is bodily organs, that is, the bodily senses (and the brain), that provide the material that the intellect understands. In this life, all our knowledge is drawn from the senses, but the intellect can understand the essences or natures of the things that are sensed. The intellect is said to abstract that essence out of what the senses present to it. Aquinas does not say much (if anything) about the brain, but it is on the side of the senses in the great distinction between sense and intellect. The brain processes and organizes information from the senses, but it does not think; that is the job of the intellect.

I, q. 75, a. 4
ARTICLE 4 — Whether the soul is man?

I answer that, The assertion "the soul is man," can be taken in two senses. First, that man is a soul; though this particular man, Socrates, for instance, is not a soul, but composed of soul and body. I say this, forasmuch as some held that the form alone belongs to the species; while matter is part of the individual, and not of the species. This cannot be true; for to the nature of the species belongs what the definition signifies; and in natural things the definition does not signify the form only, but the form and the matter. Hence in natural things the matter is part of the species; not, indeed, signate matter, which is the principle of individuality; but the common matter. For as it belongs to the notion of this particular man to be composed of this soul, of this flesh, and of these bones; so it belongs to the notion of man to be composed of soul, flesh, and bones; for whatever belongs in common to the substance of all the individuals contained under a given species, must belong also to the substance of the species. . . .

COMMENTARY

The point of this article is that the body is truly part of human nature. Man is not his soul only, but a union, or composite, of body and soul. The body was created by God and is good, and death is not to be seen as a liberation from the prison of the body, as perhaps Plato thought. This is very much in line with the Christian belief in the resurrection of the body at the Last Judgment. Man is meant to live forever in heaven as a union of body and soul, just as Jesus has His human body in heaven (and so does Mary, according to the belief of Catholics).

The bottom line is this: a soul without a body is not a human being or person; only a soul united to its body is a human being or person.

I, q. 75, a. 6
ARTICLE 6 — Whether the human soul is incorruptible?

I answer that, We must assert that the intellectual principle which we call the human soul is incorruptible. For a thing may be corrupted in two ways—per se, *and accidentally. Now it is impossible for any substance to be generated or corrupted accidentally, that is, by the generation or corruption of something else. For generation and corruption belong to a thing, just as existence belongs to it, which is acquired by generation and lost by corruption. Therefore, whatever has existence* per se *cannot be generated or corrupted except* per se; *while things which do not subsist, such as accidents and material forms, acquire existence or lose it through the generation or corruption of composite things. Now it was shown above (aa. 2, 3) that the souls of brutes are not self-subsistent, whereas the human soul is; so that the souls of brutes are corrupted; while the human soul could not be corrupted unless it were corrupted* per se. *This, indeed, is impossible, not only as regards the human soul, but also as regards anything subsistent that is a form alone. For it is clear that what belongs to a thing by virtue of itself is inseparable from it; but existence belongs to a form, which is an act, by virtue of itself. Wherefore matter acquires actual existence as it acquires the form; while it is corrupted so far as the form is separated from it. But it is impossible for a form to be separated from itself; and therefore it is impossible for a subsistent form to cease to exist.*

. . . Moreover we may take a sign of this from the fact that everything naturally aspires to existence after its own manner. Now, in things that have knowledge, desire ensues upon knowledge. The senses indeed do not know existence, except under the conditions of here *and* now, *whereas the intellect apprehends existence absolutely,*

and for all time; so that everything that has an intellect naturally desires always to exist. But a natural desire cannot be in vain. Therefore every intellectual substance is incorruptible.

COMMENTARY

The human soul is incorruptible, a fact that follows from its subsistent and incorporeal nature. This article is hard to follow, but the essential idea is that because the human soul is subsistent, it is the subject of existence, an existence which it shares with—or gives to—the body. In brute animals, it is the composite, the soul and body together, that is the true subject of existence. So, for the human soul, separation from the body does not rob it of existence, as opposed to brute animals, where death brings about the corruption of both soul and body. Hence, the human soul is incorruptible by its nature. This is also clear if one thinks of the soul as an incorporeal and immaterial subsistent thing. Such a thing is simple in a way that material and bodily things are not. Bodily things corrupt by breaking down into parts. But an immaterial, subsistent thing cannot break down into parts in that way since it has no material parts (though the human soul is not as simple as God Himself, since the human soul is not identical with its existence). And as Aquinas says in the reply to objection 1, the human soul is something that has to be directly created by God, whereas other kinds of souls arise from the natural, bodily process of generation or reproduction. This is a good indication of its incorruptibility.

One other indication of the human soul's incorruptibility is stated by Aquinas in the reply, namely, the natural desire in man to go on existing forever. Natural desires are never in vain; they always have an object that is real. We desire food; there is such a thing as food. We desire to exist forever; so we shall. We desire to know the causes of all things; there is such a thing as heaven where we will behold God.

CHAPTER THREE

ETHICS:
HAPPINESS AND VIRTUE

I–II, q. 1, a. 1
(which means the first part of the second part—
prima secundae in Latin—question 1, article 1)

QUESTION 1 — **Of man's last end**

ARTICLE 1 — **Whether it belongs to man to act for an end?**

I answer that, Of actions done by man those alone are properly called human, which are proper to man as man. Now man differs from irrational animals in this, that he is master of his actions. Wherefore those actions alone are properly called human, of which man is master. Now man is master of his actions through his reason and will; whence, too, the free-will is defined as "the faculty and will of reason." Therefore those actions are properly called human which proceed from a deliberate will. And if any other actions are found in man, they can be called actions of a man, but not properly human actions, since they are not proper to man as man. Now it is clear that whatever actions proceed from a power, are caused by that power in accordance with the nature of its object. But the object of the will is the end and the good. Therefore all human actions must be for an end.

COMMENTARY

Aquinas distinguishes between *human acts* and *acts of a man*. The former are those over which man is master, those that proceed from his intellect and will, that are deliberate and free. The *will* is simply intellectual desire, the desire that follows upon what is known by the intellect. "Human acts" are opposed to acts that are done unthinkingly—"acts of a man"—for example, stroking one's beard without even noticing that one is doing it.

It belongs to man to act for an end because that simply means that man is acting for or seeking some good, and *end* and good are basically synonymous here. The object of the will is some good, and this is also the will's end. Since all human actions proceed from the will, so all human actions are directed to some end or good.

I–II, q. 1, a. 4

ARTICLE 4 — **Whether there is one last end of human life?**

I answer that, Absolutely speaking, it is not possible to proceed indefinitely in the matter of ends, from any point of view. For in whatsoever things there is an essential order of one to another, if the first be removed, those that are ordained to the first, must of necessity be removed also. Wherefore the Philosopher proves (Phys. viii.5) that we cannot proceed to infinitude in causes of movement, because then there would be no first mover, without which neither can the others move, since they move only through being moved by the first mover. Now there is to be observed a twofold order in ends, —the order of intention, and the order of execution: and in either of these orders there must be something first. For that which is first in the order of intention, is the principle, as it were, moving the appetite; consequently, if you remove this principle, there will be nothing to move the appetite. On the other hand, the principle in execution is that wherein operation has its beginning; and if this principle be taken away, no one will begin to work. Now the principle in the intention is the last end; while the principle in execution is the first of the things which are ordained to the end. Consequently, on neither side is it possible to go on to infinity; since if there were no last end, nothing would be desired, nor would any action have its term, nor would the intention of the agent be at rest; while if there is no first thing among those that are ordained to the end, none would begin to work at anything, and counsel would have no term, but would continue indefinitely.

COMMENTARY

The reasoning in this article is similar to that we encountered in the Five Ways, where a certain type of infinite regress in causes was denied, namely, one that would not allow for a first or uncaused cause of motion or existence. Here, an infinite regress in the ends that are sought by the human being are denied, since if there were no ultimate end, then one would not begin to act. One can act for ends that are subordinate to further ends, but unless there is an ultimate end which is not ordered to a further end (that is, which is not also a means to a further end), then no initial action for an end will take place; there will be no initial desire for an end on the part of the will.

I–II, q. 1, a. 6

ARTICLE 6 — **Whether man wills all, whatsoever he wills, for the last end?**

Objection 3. Further, whoever ordains something to an end, thinks of that end. But man does not always think of the last end in all that he desires or does. Therefore man neither desires nor does all for the last end.

On the contrary, *Augustine says (De Civ. Dei xix.1): "That is the end of our good, for the sake of which we love other things, whereas we love it for its own sake."*

I answer that, Man must, of necessity, desire all, whatsoever he desires, for the last end. This is evident for two reasons. First, because whatever man desires, he desires it under the aspect of good. And if he desire it, not as his perfect good, which is the last end, he must, of necessity, desire it as tending to the perfect good, because the beginning of anything is always ordained to its completion; as is clearly the case in effects both of nature and of art. Wherefore every beginning of perfection is ordained to complete perfection which is achieved through the last end. Secondly, because the last end stands in the same relation in moving the appetite, as the first mover in other movements. Now it is clear that secondary moving causes do not move save inasmuch as they are moved by the first mover. Therefore secondary objects of the appetite do not move the appetite, except as ordained to the first object of the appetite, which is the last end.

__Reply to Objection 3__. One need not always be thinking of the last end, whenever one desires or does something: but the virtue of the first intention, which was in respect of the last end, remains in every desire directed to any object whatever, even though one's thought be not actually directed to the last end. Thus while walking along the road one needs not to be thinking of the end at every step.

Commentary

It is fairly obvious that man wills his ultimate end (at least in a general way) whenever he wills anything. If he wills something that is not the ultimate end, then he wills that good as a means to the ultimate end. All of his acts are directed to that ultimate end, which turns out to be *happiness*. And this makes sense to us, since we do everything we do because we think it will make us happy, even if we don't explicitly think of achieving happiness at every moment. Moreover, this article also makes the point that we always will things under the aspect of good; even sinful things are willed and chosen because of the good that is inherent in them, because of their good aspects. We never choose evil for the sake of evil; when we sin, we choose good things in a disordered way.

CHAPTER THREE — ETHICS: HAPPINESS AND VIRTUE

I–II, q. 1, a. 7

ARTICLE 7 — **Whether all men have the same last end?**

Objection 1. It would seem that all men have not the same last end. For before all else the unchangeable good seems to be the last end of man. But some turn away from the unchangeable good, by sinning. Therefore all men have not the same last end.

I answer that, We can speak of the last end in two ways: first, considering only the aspect of the last end; secondly, considering the thing in which the aspect of last end is realized. So, then, as to the aspect of the last end, all agree in desiring the last end: since all desire the fulfillment of their perfection, and it is precisely this fulfillment in which the last end consists, as stated above (a. 5). But as to the thing in which this aspect is realized, all men are not agreed as to their last end: since some desire riches, as their consummate good; some, pleasure; others, something else. Thus to every taste the sweet is pleasant; but to some, the sweetness of wine is most pleasant, to others, the sweetness of honey, or of something similar. Yet that sweet is absolutely the best of all pleasant things, in which he who has the best taste takes most pleasure. In like manner that good is most complete which the man with well-disposed affections desires for his last end.

Reply to Objection 1. Those who sin turn from that in which their last end really consists: but they do not turn away from the intention of the last end, which intention they mistakenly seek in other things.

COMMENTARY

All men, by virtue of their nature as men, have the same last end: happiness. All men are made to seek and find happiness, which is the same as finding man's perfection, fulfillment, or flourishing. And, in fact, it is true for all men that true happiness, the ultimate end, is found in God. But there is a sense in which the last end is not the same in all men, that is, that different men *think* that they will find happiness in different places. Some think they will find it in riches, some in power, some in honor, and so on.

I–II, q. 2, a. 8
QUESTION 2 — Of those things in which man's happiness consists
ARTICLE 8 — Whether any created good constitutes man's happiness?

I answer that, It is impossible for any created good to constitute man's happiness. For happiness is the perfect good, which lulls the appetite altogether; else it would not be the last end, if something yet remained to be desired. Now the object of the will, i.e., of man's appetite, is the universal good; just as the object of the intellect is the universal true. Hence it is evident that naught can lull man's will, save the universal good. This is to be found, not in any creature, but in God alone; because every creature has goodness by participation. Wherefore God alone can satisfy the will of man, according to the words of Ps 102:5:[1] *"Who satisfieth thy desire with good things." Therefore God alone constitutes man's happiness.*

COMMENTARY

The will's object is ultimately the universal good, unlimited and perfect good. Now, no created thing is the universal and perfect good because each created thing is a limited thing that has a limited share in goodness. The universal good can only be found in God, and only He can fulfill and satisfy the will. In fact, once someone goes to heaven and knows God in the beatific vision, then the will's enjoyment of the universal good is necessarily achieved. And the will is so satisfied by the universal good that, for Aquinas, it cannot turn away from that good. The person in heaven loses his ability to choose against God because his will is perfectly fulfilled. In this life, however, because we

---

[1] Psalm 103:5 according to current numbering.

do not have the kind of knowledge of God that will be given to us in the beatific vision, we are able to treat God as another limited good. And any limited good can be looked at from different perspectives, a perspective from which the good is attractive and a perspective which focuses on the limitation of the thing, as not as good as something else, and therefore as something to be shunned. Think for example of food, which is certainly good, but has its downside, if, say, we take into account the fact that while we are eating, we cannot do other things we would like to do; so, food is something that only partially satisfies the will and can be rejected in certain circumstances when a higher good is at stake (for example, when one fasts as a sacrifice offered to God). This ability to be attracted by and to shun created, limited goods is the root of our freedom to choose in this life. In the presence of the universal good apprehended and loved, this sort of freedom of choice would not apply.

I–II, q. 3, a. 4

QUESTION 3 — What is happiness

ARTICLE 4 — Whether, if happiness is in the intellective part, it is an operation of the intellect or the will?

Objection 4. Further, if happiness be an operation, it must needs be man's most excellent operation. But the love of God, which is an act of the will, is a more excellent operation than knowledge, which is an operation of the intellect, as the Apostle declares (1 Cor 13). Therefore it seems that happiness consists in an act of the will.

On the contrary, Our Lord said (Jn 17:3): "This is eternal life: that they may know Thee, the only true God." Now eternal life is the last end, as stated above (a. 2, ad 1).[2] Therefore man's happiness consists in the knowledge of God, which is an act of the intellect.

---

[2] When Aquinas says "ad 1" he means the reply to the first objection, in Latin *ad primum*, as in "to the first objection it must be replied".

I answer that, As stated above (q. 2, a. 6) *two things are needed for happiness: one, which is the essence of happiness: the other, that is, as it were, its proper accident, i.e., the delight connected with it. I say, then, that as to the very essence of happiness, it is impossible for it to consist in an act of the will. For it is evident from what has been said (aa.1, 2; q. 2, a. 7) that happiness is the attainment of the last end. But the attainment of the end does not consist in the very act of the will. For the will is directed to the end, both absent, when it desires it; and present, when it is delighted by resting therein. Now it is evident that the desire itself of the end is not the attainment of the end, but is a movement towards the end: while delight comes to the will from the end being present; and not conversely, is a thing made present, by the fact that the will delights in it. Therefore, that the end be present to him who desires it, must be due to something else than an act of the will.*

This is evidently the case in regard to sensible ends. For if the acquisition of money were through an act of the will, the covetous man would have it from the very moment that he wished for it. But at that moment it is far from him; and he attains it, by grasping it in his hand, or in some like manner; and then he delights in the money got. And so it is with an intelligible end. For at first we desire to attain an intelligible end; we attain it, through its being made present to us by an act of the intellect; and then the delighted will rests in the end when attained.

*So, therefore, the essence of happiness consists in an act of the intellect: but the delight that results from happiness pertains to the will. In this sense Augustine says (*Conf. x.23*) that happiness is "joy in truth," because, to wit, joy itself is the consummation of happiness.*

Reply to Objection 4. *Love ranks above knowledge in moving, but knowledge precedes love in attaining: for "naught is loved save what is known," as Augustine says (*De Trin. x.1*). Consequently we first attain an intelligible end by an act of the intellect; just as we first attain a sensible end by an act of sense.*

Chapter Three — Ethics: Happiness and Virtue

Commentary

The essence of happiness consists in an operation of the intellect because it is the intellect that makes the universal good present to the will. It is the intellect that brings about the soul's possession of the last end, and the will's enjoyment follows upon that as a proper accident, or property. A *property*, according to the technical philosophical definition, is a characteristic that a kind of thing always has, something that is not strictly part of the essence of the thing, but which necessarily flows from the essence. An example from geometry is the property of every triangle having angles equal to 180 degrees; this flows from the essence of a triangle but is not part of the essence.

This placing of the essence of happiness in an operation of the intellect follows from Aquinas's general tendency to exalt the intellect over the will as the most important and dignified part of the human being. Other medieval thinkers (usually Franciscans, while Aquinas was a Dominican) tended to exalt the will over the intellect, and therefore would have thought of the essence of happiness as the love or enjoyment of God on the part of the will.

Certainly, as the objection and the reply make clear, the love of God is more important in this life than knowledge, since love moves us toward God, toward heaven. But in heaven, we "take possession" of God with the intellect, then love what we know. So the intellect has primacy when it comes to the attainment of our last end.

I–II, q. 3, a. 5

Article 5 — Whether happiness is an operation of the speculative, or of the practical intellect?

Objection 2. Further, happiness is man's perfect good. But the practical intellect is ordained to the good rather than the speculative intellect, which is ordained to the true. Hence we are said to be good, in reference to the perfection of the practical intellect, but not in reference to the perfection to the speculative intellect, according to which we are said to be knowing or understanding.

Therefore man's happiness consists in an act of the practical intellect rather than of the speculative.

On the contrary, *Augustine says (De Trin. i.8) that "contemplation is promised us, as being the goal of all our actions, and the everlasting perfection of our joys."*

I answer that, *Happiness consists in an operation of the speculative rather than of the practical intellect. This is evident for three reasons. First because if man's happiness is an operation, it must needs be man's highest operation. Now man's highest operation is that of his highest power in respect of its highest object: and his highest power is the intellect, whose highest object is the Divine Good, which is the object, not of the practical, but of the speculative intellect. Consequently happiness consists principally in such an operation, viz., in the contemplation of Divine things. And since that "seems to be each man's self, which is best in him," according to Ethic. ix.8, and x.7, therefore such an operation is most proper to man and most delightful to him.*

Secondly, it is evident from the fact that contemplation is sought principally for its own sake. But the act of the practical intellect is not sought for its own sake but for the sake of action: and these very actions are ordained to some end. Consequently it is evident that the last end cannot consist in the active life, which pertains to the practical intellect.

Thirdly, it is again evident, from the fact that in the contemplative life man has something in common with things above him, viz., with God and the angels, to whom he is made like by happiness. But in things pertaining to the active life, other animals also have something in common with man, although imperfectly.

Therefore the last and perfect happiness, which we await in the life to come, consists entirely in contemplation. But imperfect happiness, such as can be had here, consists first and principally in contemplation, but secondly, in an operation of the practical intellect directing human actions and passions, as stated in Ethic. x.7, 8.

Reply to Objection 2. *The practical intellect is ordained to good which is outside of it: but the speculative intellect has good within it, viz., the contemplation of truth. And if this good be perfect, the whole man is perfected and made good thereby: such a good the practical intellect has not; but it directs man thereto.*

COMMENTARY

Happiness is an operation of the *speculative* intellect. This reply turns on the distinction between the intellect viewed as seeking to know the truth simply for its own sake and not for any further end—that is, speculative—and the intellect viewed as seeking to know the truth for the sake of directing some further action—that is, *practical*. The Aristotelian tradition in which Aquinas writes finds more dignity and worth in the speculative intellect. The speculative operation of the intellect is a good candidate for the last end since it is engaged in for its own sake and not for the sake of some further end, which is the key characteristic of the last end itself. Moreover, speculative knowing is seen as the highest operation of the highest faculty of man grasping the highest objects, which, again, is fitting for something that might be considered the last end. And it is speculative reason that aims to know God—obviously the highest object of knowledge—simply for the sake of knowing God. God certainly is not the object of the practical intellect, that is, something to be known for the sake of some further action beyond the knowing and its attendant loving; God is surely not a means to a further end. Finally, speculative knowing is the most divine-like thing man can do, the way he can best imitate God according to his inborn faculties. It is man's way of participating in God's own knowledge of Himself, especially as it is granted to man in the Beatific Vision. For these reasons, happiness, the last end, is seen to be an operation of the speculative intellect. Please note, however, that the speculative intellect and practical intellect are not two intellects or faculties within the human soul, but one intellect looked at from two different perspectives; one intellect is able to function both speculatively and practically.

I–II, q. 3, a. 8

ARTICLE 8 — Whether man's happiness consists in the vision of the divine essence?

On the contrary, It is written (1 Jn 3:2): "When He shall appear, we shall be like to Him; and [Vulg., because] we shall see Him as He is."

I answer that, Final and perfect happiness can consist in nothing else than the vision of the Divine Essence. To make this clear, two points must be observed. First, that man is not perfectly happy, so long as something remains for him to desire and seek: secondly, that the perfection of any power is determined by the nature of its object. Now the object of the intellect is "what a thing is," i.e., the essence of a thing, according to De Anima *iii.6. Wherefore the intellect attains perfection, in so far as it knows the essence of a thing. If therefore an intellect knows the essence of some effect, whereby it is not possible to know the essence of the cause, i.e., to know of the cause* what it is; *that intellect cannot be said to reach that cause simply, although it may be able to gather from the effect the knowledge that the cause is. Consequently, when man knows an effect, and knows that it has a cause, there naturally remains in man the desire to know about that cause,* what it is. *And this desire is one of wonder, and causes inquiry, as is stated in the beginning of the* Metaphysics *(i.2). For instance, if a man, knowing the eclipse of the sun, consider that it must be due to some cause, and know not what that cause is, he wonders about it, and from wondering proceeds to inquire. Nor does this inquiry cease until he arrive at a knowledge of the essence of the cause.*

If therefore the human intellect, knowing the essence of some created effect, knows no more of God than that He is; the perfection of that intellect does not yet reach simply the First Cause, but there remains in it the natural desire to seek the cause. Wherefore it is not yet perfectly happy. Consequently, for perfect happiness the intellect needs to reach the very Essence of the First Cause. And thus it will have its perfection through union with God as with that object, in which alone man's happiness consists, as stated above (aa. 1,7; q. 2, a. 8).

COMMENTARY

Only a knowledge of the essence of God, what God is, can be man's ultimate end, can quiet and satisfy man's longing. Philosophical knowledge of God in this life by way of effect-to-cause reasoning attains the knowledge *that* God is, but knowledge of *what* God is, is denied to us in this life. In heaven, however, we will know the essence of God, the cause of everything that exists and the fullness of Beauty, Truth, and Goodness. That kind of knowledge—and the love that flows from it—is man's ultimate good and goal, man's perfect happiness.

I–II, q. 58, a. 2

QUESTION 58 — Of the difference between moral and intellectual virtues

ARTICLE 2 — Whether moral virtue differs from intellectual virtue?

On the Contrary, It is stated in Ethic. *i.13 that "there are two kinds of virtue: some we call intellectual; some, moral."*

*I answer that, Reason is the first principle of all human acts; and whatever other principles of human acts may be found, they obey reason somewhat, but in various ways. For some obey reason blindly and without any contradiction whatever: such are the limbs of the body, provided they be in a healthy condition, for as soon as reason commands, the hand or the foot proceeds to action. Hence the Philosopher says (*Polit. *i.3) that "the soul rules the body like a despot," i.e., as a master rules a slave, who has no right to rebel. Accordingly some held that all the active principles in man are subordinate to reason in this way. If this were true, for man to act well it would suffice that his reason be perfect. Consequently,* *since virtue is a habit perfecting man in view of his doing good actions, it would follow that it is only in the reason, so that there would be none but intellectual virtues. This was the opinion of Socrates, who said "every virtue is a kind of prudence," as stated in* Ethic. vi.13. *Hence he maintained that as long as a man is in possession of knowledge, he cannot sin; and that every one who sins, does so through ignorance.*

*Now this is based on a false supposition. Because the appetitive faculty obeys the reason, not blindly, but with a certain power of opposition; wherefore the Philosopher says (*Politic. i.3*) that "reason commands the appetitive faculty by a politic power." whereby a man rules over subjects that are free, having a certain right of opposition. Hence Augustine says on Ps 118 (serm. viii) that "sometimes we understand [what is right] while desire is slow or follows not at all," in so far as the habits or passions of the appetitive faculty cause the use of reason to be impeded in some particular action. And in this way, there is some truth in the saying of Socrates that so long as a man is in possession of knowledge he does not sin: provided, however, that this knowledge is made to include the use of reason in this individual act of choice.*

Accordingly for a man to do a good deed, it is requisite not only that his reason be well disposed by means of a habit of intellectual virtue; but also that his appetite be well disposed by means of a habit of moral virtue. And so moral differs from intellectual virtue, even as the appetite differs from the reason. Hence just as the appetite is the principle of human acts, in so far as it partakes of reason, so are moral habits to be considered virtues in so far as they are in conformity with reason.

COMMENTARY

Earlier, in questions 55–56, Aquinas has attempted to define *virtue*, and a good working definition of virtue is this: a good operative habit (we might also describe virtue as "the perfection of a power" [q. 56, a. 1]). *Habit* here does not mean the automatic and unthinking behavior

CHAPTER THREE — ETHICS: HAPPINESS AND VIRTUE

we tend to think of, for example, chewing one's nails; it has more the meaning of inclination or disposition that does not exclude, but involves, thinking, deliberation, and choice. So, virtue means an inclination (habit) that a power of a soul has to act (operative) in good ways, that is, in ways that lead toward man's end. For a power to be perfected by a virtue means that it will be easier for the man to do good works through the operation of that power; virtue introduces an inclination toward—an ease and pleasure in engaging in—good actions. The opposite of virtue, vice, would mean an inclination toward evil action, an ease in performing such actions. *Vice* might be adequately defined as a bad operative habit.

Both virtue and vice, if we speak of the natural course of things, are acquired through repeated good or bad action. Repeated good action on the part of a power will result in the building up of virtue, so that good actions become "second nature" to the agent. Repeated bad action tends to result in the build up of vice, so that evil actions become "second nature." It is obviously important to try to build up virtues instead of vices, and there is no way to avoid the build-up of either one or the other; we all act all the time we are awake, and those actions are either good or evil, conducive to our true end or not, and so we are always either growing in virtue or growing in vice. This, of course, is only taking into account naturally acquired virtues, abstracting from God's grace and supernatural virtues, which Aquinas touches on later.

In this article, Aquinas is at pains to distinguish *moral* from *intellectual virtues*, virtues that perfect the appetites, on the one hand, and virtues that perfect the intellect, on the other. Some ancient thinkers, namely, Socrates, thought that only the intellect needed virtue because wrongdoing was only a matter of ignorance. But that position ignores the power that appetites and desires have to rebel against reason, so that one is able to act against one's better knowledge, to do something wrong even though, in some sense, one is not ignorant of what is right. Hence, the appetites, both those that flow from sense knowledge and those that flow from intellectual knowledge, need to be perfected by virtues so that the appetites will obey the dictates of reason.

Finally, in article 3, he shows that virtue is adequately divided into moral and intellectual. All human action springs from those two sources, intellect and appetite, so all virtues perfect one or the other. Hence, all virtues fit into one category or the other.

I–II, q. 58, a. 4

ARTICLE 4 — Whether there can be moral without intellectual virtue?

I answer that, Moral virtue can be without some of the intellectual virtues, viz., wisdom, science, and art; but not without understanding and prudence. Moral virtue cannot be without prudence, because it is a habit of choosing, i.e., making us choose well. Now in order that a choice be good, two things are required. First, that the intention be directed to a due end; and this is done by moral virtue, which inclines the appetitive faculty to the good that is in accord with reason, which is a due end. Secondly, that man take rightly those things which have reference to the end: and this he cannot do unless his reason counsel, judge, and command aright, which is the function of prudence and the virtues annexed to it, as stated above (q. 57, aa. 5, 6). Wherefore there can be no moral virtue without prudence: and consequently neither can there be without understanding. For it is by the virtue of understanding that we know self-evident principles both in speculative and in practical matters. Consequently just as right reason in speculative matters, in so far as it proceeds from naturally known principles, presupposes the understanding of those principles, so also does prudence, which is right reason about things to be done.

COMMENTARY

There can be no moral virtue, virtue that perfects appetite, without intellectual virtue (which perfects the intellect), or at least without the main intellectual virtue in practical affairs, namely, prudence (as well as a basic understanding of self-evident practical principles). Aquinas defines *prudence* as right reason about things to be done. It is the intellectual virtue that inclines the intellect to see what needs to be done here and now in order to reach man's goal of happiness. On one hand, it is the function of the appetites to desire the end to be achieved. And on the other hand, if the acting person does not have prudence, he won't see how to reach the goal he desires. Now, moral virtue concerns making good choices, choices which lead to the end, which obviously concerns choosing means to the end. But this depends on seeing the correct means, which is the province of practical reason perfected by prudence. Without prudence, therefore, there can be no moral virtue.

I–II, q. 58, a. 5

ARTICLE 5 — **Whether there can be intellectual virtue without moral virtue?**

> *Objection 2. Further, morals are the matter of prudence, even as things makeable are the matter of art. Now art can be without its proper matter, as a smith without iron. Therefore prudence can be without the moral virtues, although of all the intellectual virtues, it seems most akin to the moral virtues.*
>
> *I answer that*, *Other intellectual virtues can, but prudence cannot, be without moral virtue. The reason for this is that prudence is the right reason about things to be done (and this, not merely in general, but also in particular); about which things actions are. Now right reason demands principles from which reason proceeds to argue. And when reason argues about particular cases, it needs not only universal but also particular principles. As to universal principles of action, man is rightly disposed by the natural understanding of principles, whereby he understands that he should do no evil; or again by some practical science. But this is not enough in order that man may reason aright about particular cases. For it happens sometimes that the aforesaid universal principle, known by means of understanding or science, is destroyed in*

a particular case by a passion: thus to one who is swayed by concupiscence, when he is overcome thereby, the object of his desire seems good, although it is opposed to the universal judgment of his reason. Consequently, as by the habit of natural understanding or of science, man is made to be rightly disposed in regard to the universal principles of action; so, in order that he be rightly disposed with regard to the particular principles of action, viz., the ends, he needs to be perfected by certain habits, whereby it becomes connatural, as it were, to man to judge aright to the end. This is done by moral virtue: for the virtuous man judges aright of the end of virtue, because "such as a man is, such does the end seem to him" (Ethic. iii.5). Consequently the right reason about things to be done, viz., prudence, requires man to have moral virtue.

Reply to Objection 2. *It does not depend on the disposition of our appetite whether we judge well or ill of the principles of art, as it does, when we judge of the end which is the principle in moral matters: in the former case our judgment depends on reason alone. Hence art does not require a virtue perfecting the appetite, as prudence does.*

Commentary

Here, we have the flip-side of the previous question, and the answer shows the interconnection between moral and intellectual virtue; one simply cannot exist without the other, at least as regards prudence. If man is to judge correctly what is to be done here and now, he needs prudence. But in order for the appetites to be governable by reason, so that they don't rear up and go against what reason knows to be right, moral virtue is needed, that perfection of the appetites that keeps them in check and open to reason's governance. If the appetites aren't so trained, they are apt to lead to wrongdoing, to unreasonable action. But unreasonable action is obviously contrary to prudence. So appetites unperfected by moral virtue make it impossible for prudence to exist. Or, to look at it in a slightly different way, moral virtues provide necessary help to prudence by bringing about the proper desires, by ensuring that the appetites have the right object, the right end, which makes good, prudent choices "connatural" to man—that is, "second nature," or easy and pleasant. Without that proper orientation within the appetites, the right reason about things to be done, namely, prudence, cannot exist, because unruly appetites or passions will destroy it; practical reason will only be deliberating about means to a bad end, which may be "clever" but cannot rightfully be called "prudent." Hence, prudence cannot exist without moral virtue, and one must practice and try to build both moral and intellectual virtue at the same time.

The reply to the objection is useful for making clear the difference between prudence and art, where art—right reason about things to be *made*—is purely concerned with the intellect, while prudence—right reason about things to be *done*—though a perfection of the intellect, has a necessary connection with, and dependence upon, moral virtues that perfect the appetites. Such distinctions help one to understand, since the human mind especially profits from contrasts.

I–II, q. 61, a. 2

QUESTION 61 — Of the cardinal virtues
ARTICLE 2 — Whether there are four cardinal virtues?

I answer that, Things may be numbered either in respect of their formal principles, or according to the subjects in which they are: and either way we find that there are four cardinal virtues.

For the formal principle of the virtue of which we speak now is good as defined by reason; which good can be considered in two ways. First, as existing in the very act of reason: and thus we have one principal virtue, called Prudence.—*Secondly, according as the reason puts its order into something else; either into operations, and then we have* Justice; *or into passions, and then we need two virtues. For the need of putting the order of reason into the passions is due to their thwarting reason: and this occurs in two ways. First, by the passions inciting to something against reason; and then the passions need a curb, which we call* Temperance. *Secondly, by the passions withdrawing us from following the dictate of reason, e.g., through fear of danger or toil: and then man needs to be strengthened for that which reason dictates, lest he turn back; and to this end there is* Fortitude.

In like manner, we find the same number if we consider the subjects of virtue. For there are four subjects of the virtue we speak of now: viz., the power which is rational in its essence, and this is perfected by Prudence; *and that which is rational by participation, and is threefold, the will, subject of* Justice; *the concupiscible faculty, subject of* Temperance; *and the irascible faculty, subject of* Fortitude.

COMMENTARY

Cardinal virtues are those that are the most necessary for a good human life, the "hinges" (from Latin, *cardo, cardinis*) upon which the moral life turns. There are four cardinal virtues, as enumerated by Aquinas and by a long tradition preceding him: prudence, justice, temperance, and fortitude. *Prudence*, as we have seen, is the virtue perfecting the practical intellect so that it reasons rightly about things to be done. *Justice* perfects the will in its operations so that it acts according to reason in desiring and giving to others, including God, what is right and due. *Temperance* perfects the passions, or the concupiscible appetite, the desire for pleasure, so that that desire does not go beyond what reason ordains. And *fortitude* perfects the desire for goods that are difficult to obtain, goods that are threatened by some obstacle (sometimes even death); this virtue perfects, therefore, what is called the irascible appetite and keeps one from falling away from what is good because of difficulties or threats. These are the virtues that lie at the foundation of man's search for happiness; he cannot achieve his ultimate end without them.

I–II, q. 62, a. 1

QUESTION 62 — **Of the theological virtues**

ARTICLE 1 — **Whether there are any theological virtues?**

I answer that, Man is perfected by virtue, for those actions whereby he is directed to happiness, as was explained above (q. 5, a. 7). Now man's happiness is twofold, as was also stated above (ibid., a. 5). One is proportionate to human nature, a happiness, to wit, which man can obtain by means of his natural principles. The other is a happiness surpassing man's nature, and which man can obtain by the power of God alone, by a kind of participation of the Godhead, about which it is written (2 Pet 1:4) that by Christ we are made "partakers of the divine nature." And because such happiness surpasses the capacity of human nature, man's natural principles which enable him to act well according to his capacity, do not suffice to direct man to this same happiness. Hence it is necessary for man to receive from God some additional principles, whereby he may be directed to supernatural happiness, even as he is directed to his connatural end, by means of his natural principles, albeit not without the Divine assistance. Such like principles are called theological virtues: *first, because their object is God, inasmuch as they direct us aright to God: secondly, because they are infused in us by God alone: thirdly, because these virtues are not made known to us, save by Divine revelation, contained in Holy Writ.*

COMMENTARY

Man's end is God beheld in the Beatific Vision. Virtue perfects man by perfecting the actions that lead to his ultimate end. But man's end is beyond his natural powers since it is a supernatural end. Hence, man needs supernatural virtues to direct him toward God, and these are called *theological* virtues: *faith* (by which we believe in God and

His revelation), *hope* (by which we trust God to bring us to heaven), and *charity* (by which we love God above all else and others for His sake). These virtues are called theological because (1) God is their object; (2) they are infused in us by God alone by grace and are not obtained through repeated good action as natural virtues are (charity, as defined above and without which we cannot go to heaven, is lost by mortal sin); (3) we know of them only by way of divine revelation.

CHAPTER FOUR

LAW

I–II, q. 90, prologue

QUESTION 90 — Of the essence of law

Prologue. We have now to consider the extrinsic principles of acts. Now the extrinsic principle inclining to evil is the devil, of whose temptations we have spoken in the First Part (q. 114). But the extrinsic principle moving to good is God, Who both instructs us by means of His Law, and assists us by His Grace: wherefore in the first place we must speak of law; in the second place, of grace.

I–II, q. 90, a. 1

ARTICLE 1 — Whether law is something pertaining to reason?

I answer that, Law is a rule and measure of acts, whereby man is induced to act or is restrained from acting: for lex (law) is derived from ligare (to bind), because it binds one to act. Now the rule and measure of human acts is the reason, which is the first principle of human acts, as is evident from what has been stated above (q. 1, a. 1, ad. 3); since it belongs to the reason to direct to the end, which is the first principle in all matters of action, according to the Philosopher (*Phys. ii*). Now that which is the principle in any genus, is the rule and measure of that *genus: for instance, unity in the genus of numbers, and the first movement in the genus of movements. Consequently it follows that law is something pertaining to reason.*

Commentary

Law comes from reason and not primarily from the will. This is so because it belongs to reason to direct actions to the ultimate end. If law came primarily from the will, then the law would be essentially something arbitrary and merely posited. But if it comes from reason, then it is something rational, something that objectively—that is, in accordance with reality, or the way things are—directs us towards goodness and happiness; the law is truly for our own good and is not there to keep us "down" or in shackles.

I–II, q. 90, a. 2

ARTICLE 2 — **Whether law is always something directed to the common good?**

*On the contrary, Isidore says (*Etym. v.21*) that "laws are enacted for no private profit, but for the common benefit of the citizens."*

I answer that, As stated above (a. 1), the law belongs to that which is a principle of human acts, because it is their rule and measure. Now as reason is a principle of human acts, so in reason itself there is something which is the principle in respect of all the rest: wherefore to this principle chiefly and mainly law must needs be referred.—Now the first principle in practical matters, which are the object of the practical reason, is the last end: and the last end of human life is bliss or happiness, as stated above (q. 2, a. 7; q. 3, a. 1). Consequently the law must needs regard principally the relationship to happiness. Moreover, since every part is ordained to the whole, as imperfect to perfect; and since one man is a part of the perfect community, the law must needs regard properly the relationship to universal happiness. Wherefore the

*Philosopher, in the above definition of legal matters mentions both happiness and the body politic: for he says (*Ethic. v.1*) that we call those legal matters "just, which are adapted to produce and preserve happiness and its parts for the body politic": since the state is a perfect community, as he says in* Polit. i.1.

Now in every genus, that which belongs to it chiefly is the principle of the others, and the others belong to that genus in subordination to that thing: thus fire, which is chief among hot things, is the cause of heat in mixed bodies, and these are said to be hot in so far as they have a share of fire. Consequently, since the law is chiefly ordained to the common good, any other precept in regard to some individual work, must needs be devoid of the nature of law, save in so far as it regards the common good. Therefore every law is ordained to the common good.

COMMENTARY

Law by its nature is something connected with the common good. The point and purpose of the law is to direct human beings to their last end: happiness. But the happiness sought is not just for individuals but for human communities, and even all of humanity. Hence, law pertains to the common good: the good, flourishing, or happiness of the community.

I–II, q. 90, a. 3

ARTICLE 3 — **Whether the reason of any man is competent to make laws?**

Objection 2. *Further, as the Philosopher says (*Ethic. ii.1*), "the intention of the lawgiver is to lead men to virtue." But every man can lead another to virtue. Therefore the reason of any man is competent to make laws.*

I answer that, A law, properly speaking, regards first and foremost the order to the common good. Now to order anything to the common good, belongs either to the whole people, or to someone who is the viceregent of the whole people. And therefore the making of a law belongs either to the whole people or to a public personage who has care of the whole people: since in all other matters the directing of anything to the end concerns him to whom the end belongs.

*Reply to Objection 2. A private person cannot lead another to virtue efficaciously: for he can only advise, and if his advice be not taken, it has no coercive power, such as the law should have, in order to prove an efficacious inducement to virtue, as the Philosopher says (*Ethic. x.9*). But this coercive power is vested in the whole people or in some public personage, to whom it belongs to inflict penalties, as we shall state further on (q. 92, a. 2, ad. 3; II–II, q. 64, a. 3). Wherefore the framing of laws belongs to him alone.*

Commentary

The law directs the community toward its end. But it belongs to the community of rational agents to make the laws of the community; this means that the community is to direct itself toward its end by making its own laws. So either the community as a whole, or representatives that the community chooses, are the only ones competent to make laws, the only ones who have that right.

The objection and its reply make clear that the purpose of law is to lead to virtue, which leads to happiness. Note, therefore, the close connection between virtue and happiness; only the virtuous man is or can be happy.

I–II, q. 90, a. 4

Article 4 — **Whether promulgation is essential to a law?**

Objection 1. It would seem that promulgation is not essential to a law. For the natural law above all has the character of law.

CHAPTER FOUR — LAW 61

But the natural law needs no promulgation. Therefore it is not essential to a law that it be promulgated.

I answer that, As stated above (a. 1), a law is imposed on others by way of a rule and measure. Now a rule or measure is imposed by being applied to those who are to be ruled and measured by it. Wherefore, in order that a law obtain the binding force which is proper to a law, it must needs be applied to the men who have to be ruled by it. Such application is made by its being notified to them by promulgation. Wherefore promulgation is necessary for the law to obtain its force.

Thus from the four preceding articles, the definition of law may be gathered; and it is nothing else than an ordinance of reason for the common good, made by him who has care of the community, and promulgated.

Reply to Objection 1. The natural law is promulgated by the very fact that God instilled it into man's mind so as to be known by him naturally.

COMMENTARY

For a law to be binding, it must be known. And so a law must be promulgated, or made known, if it is to qualify as a law. The objection and the reply give us our first look at the natural law and show that it is made known to us simply by God's creating us as rational beings and writing it on our hearts (or minds). At this point, we've also reached a definition of law, a statement of its essence, which is given by Aquinas at the end of his reply.

I–II, q. 91, a. 1

Question 91 — Of the various kinds of law

ARTICLE 1 — **Whether there is an eternal law?**

I answer that, As stated above (q. 90, a. 1, ad. 2; aa. 3, 4), a law is nothing but a dictate of practical reason emanating from the ruler who governs a perfect community. Now it is evident, granted that the world is ruled by Divine Providence, as was stated in the First Part (q. 22, aa.1, 2), that the whole community of the universe is governed by Divine Reason. Wherefore the very Idea of the government of things in God the Ruler of the universe, has the nature of a law. And since the Divine Reason's conception of things is not subject to time but is eternal, according to Prov. 8:23, therefore it is that this kind of law must be called eternal.

Commentary

The first kind of law, *eternal law*, is nothing other than God's reason or mind as directing or governing His creatures to their end. How God conceives things in His mind is how they ought to be; this is the goal or end of all of creation as conceived by God. This conception of things is then the ground of His actual governance of, or providential care for, His creatures. Thus, "God's conception of things," the plan in His mind for how His creation should turn out and the end which it should attain, has the character of law.[1] This law is called eternal because God is eternal, which means altogether outside of time and the succession involved in being subject to time.

I–II, q. 91, a. 2

ARTICLE 2 — **Whether there is in us a natural law?**

I answer that, As stated above (q. 90, a. 1, ad. 1), law, being a rule and measure, can be in a person in two ways: in one way, as in him that rules and measures; in another way, as in that which is ruled and measured, since a thing is ruled and measured, in so far as it partakes of the rule or measure. Wherefore, since all

---

[1] My understanding of this passage was aided by Denis J. M. Bradley, *Aquinas on the Twofold Human Good* (Washington, D.C.: The Catholic University of America Press, 1997), 129–30.

CHAPTER FOUR — LAW   63

things subject to Divine providence are ruled and measured by the eternal law, as was stated above (a. 1); it is evident that all things partake somewhat of the eternal law, in so far as, namely, from its being imprinted on them, they derive their respective inclinations to their proper acts and ends. Now among all others, the rational creature is subject to Divine providence in the most excellent way, in so far as it partakes of a share of providence, by being provident both for itself and others. Wherefore it has a share of the Eternal Reason, whereby it has a natural inclination to its proper act and end: and this participation of the eternal law in the rational creature is called the natural law. Hence the Psalmist after saying (Ps 4:6): "Offer up the sacrifice of justice," as though someone asked what the works of justice are, adds: "Many say, who showeth us good things?" in answer to which question he says: "The light of Thy countenance, O Lord, is signed upon us": thus implying that the light of natural reason, whereby we discern what is good and what is evil, which is the function of the natural law, is nothing else than an imprint on us of the Divine light. It is therefore evident that the natural law is nothing else than the rational creature's participation of the eternal law.

COMMENTARY

The second kind of law is *natural law*. Everything other than God is subject to the eternal law. But some creatures, the rational ones, are subject to it in a special way, precisely because they are rational and can direct themselves to their ultimate end (as a kind of free cooperation with God's governing). Hence, the natural law is defined as "the rational creature's participation of [in] the eternal law." The basic idea, again, is that rational creatures can know about, and move themselves toward, happiness and flourishing; being subject to natural law means that human beings can know, apart from revelation, some of the ways they need to act and some of the ways of acting they need to avoid in order to be fulfilled and happy creatures. Such knowledge is *natural* to them, and what they can know is what is at least partially perfective of their human *nature* (two reasons why natural law has its name).

I–II, q. 91, a. 3
ARTICLE 3 — Whether there is a human law?

I answer that, As stated above (q. 90, a. 1, ad. 2), a law is a dictate of the practical reason. Now it is to be observed that the same procedure takes place in the practical and in the speculative reason: for each proceeds from principles to conclusions, as stated above (ibid.). Accordingly we conclude that just as, in the speculative reason, from naturally known indemonstrable principles, we draw the conclusions of various sciences, the knowledge of which is not imparted to us by nature, but acquired by the efforts of reason, so too it is from the precepts of the natural law, as from general and indemonstrable principles, that the human reason needs to proceed to more particular determination of certain matters. These particular determinations, devised by human reason, are called human laws, provided the other essential conditions of law be observed, as stated above (q. 90, aa. 2, 3, 4). . . .

COMMENTARY

The third kind of law is *human law*. These are the laws made up by human beings that either embody and codify precepts of the natural law or else provide some further determination or specificity to the natural law as needed. An instance of the former function of human law would be a law that forbids theft or murder, a human law that merely restates something already in the natural law. An instance of the latter function of human law would be the determination within a certain country that all vehicles should travel on the right side of the road. It is not necessary that vehicles travel on the right side, but it is necessary that one side or the other be chosen, since otherwise chaos would ensue. Hence, some determination must be made, but which particular determination is not decreed by natural law, and that determination, or act of specifying, is the province of human law. The important thing for human law is that it should reflect or be in line with the natural law, and *never at variance with it*; a human law that contradicts natural law is, in fact, no law at all.

I–II, q. 91, a. 4

ARTICLE 4 — Whether there was any need for a divine law?

I answer that, Besides the natural and the human law it was necessary for the directing of human conduct to have a Divine law. And this for four reasons. First, because it is by law that man is directed how to perform his proper acts in view of his last end. And indeed if man were ordained to no other end than that which is proportionate to his natural faculty, there would be no need for man to have any further direction on the part of his reason, besides the natural law and human law which is derived from it. But since man is ordained to an end of eternal happiness which is not proportionate to man's natural faculty, as stated above (q. 5, a. 5), therefore it was necessary that, besides the natural and the human law, man should be directed to his end by a law given by God.

Secondly, because, on account of the uncertainty of human judgment, especially on contingent and particular matters, different people form different judgments on human acts; whence also different and contrary laws result. In order, therefore, that man may know without any doubt what he ought to do and what he ought to avoid, it was necessary for man to be directed in his proper acts by a law given by God, for it is certain that such a law cannot err.

Thirdly, because man can make laws in those matters of which he is competent to judge. But man is not competent to judge of interior movements, that are hidden, but only of exterior acts which appear: and yet for the perfection of virtue it is necessary for man to conduct himself aright in both kinds of acts.

Consequently human law could not sufficiently curb and direct interior acts; and it was necessary for this purpose that a Divine law should supervene.

Fourthly, because, as Augustine says (De Lib. Arb. i.5,6), human law cannot punish or forbid all evil deeds: since while aiming at doing away with all evils, it would do away with many good things, and would hinder the advance of the common good, which is necessary for human intercourse. In order, therefore, that no evil might remain unforbidden and unpunished, it was necessary for the Divine law to supervene, whereby all sins are forbidden. . . .

COMMENTARY

The *divine law* under discussion here is basically identical to biblical law, the Old and New Covenants. This is divinely revealed law, and it was necessary for four reasons: (1) because it directs us to our supernatural end, heaven; since our end is beyond our nature, a law beyond our nature and its powers must be given to direct us to that end; (2) to provide certainty about how to act, which is often not attainable by human beings left to their own powers; (3) to provide direction about interior actions and motivations, which human law cannot direct; human law only directs external behavior, not the heart, but true virtue requires both good interior dispositions as well as good external behavior; (4) to bring completeness to what is commanded and forbidden since human law cannot be complete owing to situations where it would do more harm than good to forbid certain vices. Divine law makes up for what is lacking in human law by forbidding and commanding everything that should be commanded and forbidden according to the eternal law.

So, the divine law is God telling us parts of the eternal law that we cannot reach by human reason as well as those moral truths which human reason *can* reach. The natural law corresponds roughly to the Ten Commandments; so we can in principle know the Ten Commandments (or at least most of them, particularly those concerned with our treatment of other human beings) by reason alone, but God goes ahead and reveals it anyway to make it more certain and accessible to us.

I–II, q. 94, a. 2
Question 94 — Of the natural law
ARTICLE 2 — Whether the natural law contains several precepts or one only?

I answer that, As stated above (q. 91, a. 3), the precepts of the natural law are to the practical reason, what the first principles of demonstrations are to the speculative reason; because both are self-evident principles. Now a thing is said to be self-evident in two ways: first, in itself; secondly, in relation to us. Any proposition is said to be self-evident in itself, if its predicate is contained in the notion of its subject: although, to one who knows not the definition of the subject, it happens that such a proposition is not self-evident. For instance, this proposition, "Man is a rational being," is, in its very nature, self-evident, since he who says man, *says a* rational being: *and yet to one who knows not what a man is, this proposition is not self-evident. Hence it is that, as Boethius says (*De Hebdom.*), certain axioms or propositions are universally self-evident to all; and such are those propositions whose terms are known to all, as, "Every whole is greater than its part," and, "Things equal to one and the same are equal to one another." But some propositions are self-evident only to the wise, who understand the meaning of the terms of such propositions: thus to one who understands that an angel is not a body, it is self-evident than an angel is not circumscriptively in a place: but this is not evident to the unlearned, for they cannot grasp it.*

Now a certain order is to be found in those things that are apprehended universally. For that which, before aught else, falls under apprehension, is being, *the notion of which is included in all things whatsoever a man apprehends. Wherefore the first indemonstrable principle is that "the same thing cannot be affirmed and denied at the same time," which is based on the notion of being and not-being: and on this principle all others are based, as stated in* Metaph. *iv, text 9. Now as being is the first thing that falls under the apprehension simply, so good is the first thing that falls under the apprehension of the practical reason, which is directed to action: since every agent acts for an end under the aspect of good. Consequently the first principle in the practical reason is one founded on the notion of good, viz., that "good is that which all things seek after." Hence this is the first precept of law, that "good is to be done and pursued, and evil is to be avoided." All other precepts of the natural law are based upon this: so that whatever the practical reason naturally apprehends as man's good (or evil) belongs to the precepts of the natural law as something to be done or avoided.*

Since, however, good has the nature of an end, and evil, the nature of a contrary, hence it is that all those things to which man has a natural inclination, are naturally apprehended by reason as being good, and consequently as objects of pursuit, and their contraries as evil, and objects of avoidance. Wherefore according to the order of natural inclinations, is the order of the precepts of the natural law. Because in man there is first of all an inclination to good in accordance with the nature he has in common with all substances: inasmuch as every substance seeks the preservation of its own being, according to its nature: and by reason of this inclination, whatever is a means of preserving human life, and of warding off its obstacles, belongs to the natural law. Secondly, there is in man an inclination to things that pertain to him more specially, according to that nature which he has in common with other animals: and in virtue of this inclination, those things are said to belong to the natural law, "which nature has taught to all animals," such as sexual intercourse, education of offspring and so forth. Thirdly, there is in man an inclination to good, according to the nature of his reason, which nature is proper to him: thus man has a natural inclination to know the truth about God, and to live in society: and in this respect, whatever pertains to this inclination belongs to the natural law; for instance, to shun ignorance, to avoid offending those among whom one has to live, and other such things regarding the above inclination.

Commentary

The primary precept of the natural law, the one that, like the principle of non-contradiction, is in some way self-evidently true, is: "Do good and avoid evil." This is what we all do and what we cannot not do; even when we sin we seek after something insofar as it is appears to be good for us; we are constituted to seek the good, which therefore takes on the nature of an end (something sought). From the primary precept, the secondary precepts can be derived in conjunction with the natural inclinations found in human nature, inclinations to things that are good for, or fulfilling of, human nature.

The first inclination we come upon is something common to all creatures, namely, the inclination to continue in existence. From this comes the precept that we are to take care of ourselves, neither harming ourselves nor other innocent human beings (including the unborn), and respect life in every way (basically corresponding to the Fifth Commandment: you shall not kill). Of course, strictly speaking, the command here concerns self-preservation, but perhaps the extension to others is implied. It certainly comes to the fore later, when the inclination to live in society is discussed.

The next inclination is one shared between human beings and other animals, namely, the desire to reproduce and raise offspring. From this come the precepts regarding sexuality and marriage and the care of children; this basically corresponds to the Sixth Commandment: you shall not commit adultery. Hence, it is part of the natural law that marriage is between one man and one woman and that sex is reserved for marriage, for the rearing of human children requires a stable human family. Nor is artificial contraception allowed on the grounds that it frustrates one of the essential purposes of the sexual act: having children.

The final main inclination that we find is one that is specific to human beings, rational animals. This clearly proceeds from the fact that human beings possess reason, and it is a natural inclination to exercise that reason in knowing the truth, especially about God, and in living in society with others, which, as Aquinas spells out, means shunning ignorance and avoiding offending others. The good of living in society and knowing the truth yields all sorts of precepts corresponding to the Ten Commandments, for instance, do not kill, do not commit adultery, do not steal, do not bear false witness, and so on; all sins against these Commandments are destructive of society and go against the truth of what human beings are as God's creatures.

I–II, q. 94, a. 4

ARTICLE 4 — **Whether the natural law is the same in all men?**

I answer that, As stated above (aa. 2, 3), to the natural law belongs those things to which a man is inclined naturally: and among these it is proper to man to be inclined to act according to reason. Now the process of reason is from the common to the proper, as stated in Phys. i. *The speculative reason, however, is differently situated in this matter, from the practical reason. For, since the speculative reason is busied chiefly with necessary things, which cannot be otherwise than they are, its proper conclusions, like the universal principles, contain the truth without fail. The practical reason, on the other hand, is busied with contingent matters, about which human actions are concerned: and consequently, although there is necessity in the general principles, the more we descend to matters of detail, the more frequently we encounter defects. Accordingly then in speculative matters truth is the same in all men, both as to principles and as to conclusions: although the truth is not known to all as regards the conclusions, but only as regards the principles which are called common notions. But in matters of action, truth or practical rectitude is not the same for all, as to matters of detail, but only as to the general principles: and where there is the same rectitude in matters of detail, it is not equally known to all.*

It is therefore evident that, as regards the general principles whether of speculative or of practical reason, truth or rectitude is the same for all, and is equally known by all. As to the proper conclusions of the speculative reason, the truth is the same for all, but is not equally known to all: thus it is true for all that the three angles of a triangle are together equal to two right angles, although it is not known to all. But as to the proper conclusions of the practical reason, neither is the truth or rectitude the same for all, nor, where it is the same, is it equally known by all. Thus it is right and true for all to act according to reason: and from this principle it follows as a proper conclusion, that goods entrusted to another should be restored to their owner. Now this is true for the majority of cases: but it may happen in a particular case that it would be injurious, and therefore unreasonable, to restore goods held in trust; for instance if they are claimed for the purpose of fighting against one's country. And this principle will be found to fail the more, according as we descend further into detail, e.g., if one were to say that goods held in trust should be restored with such and such a guarantee, or in such and such a way; because the greater the number of conditions added, the greater the number of ways in which the principle may fail, so that it be not right to restore or not restore.

Consequently we must say that the natural law, as to general principles, is the same for all, both as to rectitude and as to knowledge. But as to certain matters of detail, which are conclusions, as it were, of those general principles, it is the same for all in the majority of cases, both as to rectitude and as to knowledge; and yet in some few cases it may fail, both as to rectitude, by reason of certain obstacles (just as natures subject to generation or corruption fail in some few cases on account of some obstacle), and as to knowledge, since in some the reason is perverted by passion, or evil habit, or an evil disposition of nature; thus formerly, theft, although it is expressly contrary to the natural law, was not considered wrong among the Germans, as Julius Caesar relates (De Bello Gall. vi).

COMMENTARY

The most general practical precepts are the same for all men; they are true for all men, times, and situations, and they are known by all men, especially the most general precept: "Do good and avoid evil." Certainly, the more general secondary precepts, the ones corresponding to the Ten Commandments, are true for all men and all situations, though they may not be known by all men, and this could be because of sin, passions, evil habits and customs, and so on. But the more particular the precepts become, as we formulate more particular principles that are intended to apply to complicated situations, the precepts tend to fail more often, that is, fail to be true and also fail to be known by men, because, once again, men are inclined to be evil. Aquinas gives the example of returning someone's weapons, which would usually be a good thing to do. He seems to envision this as a kind of conclusion from the more general principle that one ought to act according to reason, which is true for all men and all situations. But if the person to whom one is to return the weapons intends to use them to commit treason, then the precept that one should return such goods is not true in that case. In other words, that precept is usually, but not always, true. So as the precepts get more particular, they become less absolutely true and admit of more exceptions. And the more particular the precept, even when true and valid as applied to a situation, the more likely it is not to be known by men, because evil habits or evil customs interfere with reason even more when it comes to particular situations, which call, above all, for the exercise of prudence. For, as was stated above,[2] prudence for its very existence depends on the moral virtues, or virtues of character (particularly courage, temperance, and justice), as well as teaching and experience.

---

[2] See above I–II, q. 58, a. 5 (chapter 3, p. 51).

I–II, q. 95, a. 1

QUESTION 95 — Of human law

ARTICLE 1 — Whether it was useful for laws to be framed by men?

I answer that, As stated above (q. 63, a. 1; q. 94, a. 3), man has a natural aptitude for virtue; but the perfection of virtue must be acquired by man by means of some kind of training. Thus we observe that man is helped by industry in his necessities, for instance, in food and clothing. Certain beginnings of these he has from nature, viz., his reason and his hands; but he has not the full complement, as other animals have, to whom nature has given sufficiency of clothing and food. Now it is difficult to see how man could suffice for himself in the matter of this training: since the perfection of virtue consists chiefly in withdrawing man from undue pleasures, to which above all man is inclined, and especially the young, who are more capable of being trained. Consequently a man needs to receive this training from another, whereby to arrive at the perfection of virtue. And as to those young people who are inclined to acts of virtue, by their good natural disposition, or by custom, or rather by the gift of God, paternal training suffices, which is by admonitions. But since some are found to be depraved, and prone to vice, and not easily amenable to words, it was necessary for such to be restrained from evil by force and fear, in order that, at least, they might desist from evil-doing, and leave others in peace, and that they themselves, by being habituated in this way, might be brought to do willingly what hitherto they did from fear, and thus become virtuous. Now this kind of training, which compels through fear of punishment, is the discipline of laws. Therefore, in order that man might have peace and virtue, it was necessary for laws to be framed: for, as the Philosopher says (Polit. i.2), "as man is the most noble of animals if he be perfect in virtue, so is he the lowest of all, if he be severed from law and righteousness," because *man can use his reason to devise means of satisfying his lusts and evil passions, which other animals are unable to do.*

Commentary

The law is framed by men to train them in virtue and bring about peace in society. Often, the young receive the training they need from their parents. But some are deprived of that training—or perhaps have evil dispositions that were resistant to parental training—and thus need the training provided by the law. The law can train by restraining the evil impulses of men through force and fear. This does not immediately give men virtuous hearts, but if they begin by behaving virtuously in their external behavior, then eventually interior rectitude may come about, so that they do good willingly, easily, and with pleasure. And, of course, the law is there to bring peace and protect people from the evildoing of others.

I–II, q. 95, a. 2

Article 2 — Whether every human law is derived from the natural law?

I answer that, As Augustine says (De Lib. Arb. i.5), "that which is not just seems to be no law at all": wherefore the force of a law depends on the extent of its justice. Now in human affairs a thing is said to be just, from being right, according to the rule of reason. But the first rule of reason is the law of nature, as is clear from what has been stated above (q. 91, a. 2, ad. 2). Consequently every human law has just so much of the nature of law, as it is derived from the law of nature. But if in any point it deflects from the law of nature, it is no longer a law but a perversion of the law.

But it most be noted that something may be derived from the natural law in two ways: first, as a conclusion from premises, secondly, by way of determination of certain generalities. The

CHAPTER FOUR — LAW 75

first way is like to that by which, in sciences, demonstrated conclusions are drawn from the principles: while the second mode is likened to that whereby, in the arts, general forms are particularized as to details: thus the craftsman needs to determine the general form of a house to some particular shape. Some things are therefore derived from the general principles of the natural law, by way of conclusions; e.g., that "one must not kill" may be derived as a conclusion from the principle that "one should do harm to no man": while some are derived therefrom by way of determination; e.g., the law of nature has it that the evil-doer should be punished; but that he be punished in this or that way, is a determination of the law of nature.

Accordingly both modes of derivation are found in the human law. But those things which are derived in the first way, are contained in the human law not as emanating therefrom exclusively, but have some force from the natural law also. But those things which are derived in the second way, have no other force than that of human law.

COMMENTARY

The main point is that a human law is just, reasonable, and valid only if it is in line with the natural law. If a human law is contrary to the natural law, then it does not even have the nature of a law; it is no law at all. Conformity with the natural law is the standard of justice for all human laws.

Some human laws are derivations from the natural law in such a way that they are really part of the natural law now stated in human law, for example, laws against murder. These human laws also have the force of the natural law behind them. Some derivations of the human law from the natural law have only the force of human law; these human laws—for example, that all cars must drive on the right in the United States or the particular prison sentences attached to certain crimes—are (presumably) in line with the natural law, but they are determinations that are not exactly *part of* the natural law. Some such laws are necessary, but what they turn out to be with regard to their particular content is up to human determination alone and is not decidable by looking at the natural law.

I–II, q. 96, a. 2

QUESTION 96 — Of the power of human law

ARTICLE 2 — Whether it belongs to the human law to repress all vices?

Objection 2. *Further, the intention of the lawgiver is to make the citizens virtuous. But a man cannot be virtuous unless he forebear from all kinds of vice. Therefore it belongs to human law to repress all vices.*

I answer that, As stated above (q. 90, aa. 1, 2), law is framed as a rule or measure of human acts. Now a measure should be homogenous with that which it measures, as stated in Metaph. *x, text 3,4, since different things are measured by different measures. Wherefore laws imposed on men should also be in keeping with their condition, for, as Isidore says (*Etym. *v.21), law should be "possible both according to nature, and according to the customs of the country." Now possibility or faculty of action is due to an inferior habit or disposition: since the same thing is not possible to one who has not a virtuous habit, as is possible to one who has. Thus the same is not possible to a child as to a full-grown man: for which reason the law for children is not the same as for adults, since many things are permitted to children, which in an adult are punished by law or at any rate are open to blame. In like manner many things are permissible to men not perfect in virtue, which would be intolerable in a virtuous man.*

Now human law is framed for a number of human beings, the majority of whom are not perfect in virtue. Wherefore human laws do not forbid all vices, from which the virtuous abstain, but only the more grievous vices, from which it is possi-

> ble for the majority to abstain; and chiefly those that are to the hurt of others, without the prohibition of which human society could not be maintained: thus human law prohibits murder, theft, and suchlike.
>
> **Reply to Objection 2.** *The purpose of human law is to lead men to virtue, not suddenly, but gradually. Wherefore it does not lay upon the multitude of imperfect men the burdens of those who are already perfect in virtue, viz., that they should abstain from all evil. Otherwise these imperfect ones, being unable to bear such precepts, would break out into yet greater evils: thus it is written (Prov 30:33): "He that violently bloweth his nose, bringeth out blood"; and (Mt 9:17) that if "new wine," i.e., precepts of a perfect life, is "put into old bottles," i.e., into imperfect men, "the bottles break, and the wine runneth out," i.e., the precepts are despised, and those men, from contempt, break out into evils worse still.*

Commentary

This article shows the limits of human law, that it only forbids or represses the most grievous vices, those that the majority of people are able to abstain from, and those that most obviously and directly harm others and damage society, for example, murder and theft. To try to hold men accountable to higher standards of morality by way of human law would only make men worse, pushing them to rebel against even the most basic restraints. The purpose of law is again stated, namely, to lead men to virtue gradually—and this is the precise reason why legislation should be limited to the most necessary items—which is often not how people in this day and age view the purpose of law. They tend, rather, to see it as only a restraint that keeps people from harming others so that each one is left free to pursue his own version of the good life without interference.

GLOSSARY

Act (or actuality)—What *is*, as opposed to potency, or what *can be*.

Acts of a man—Non-deliberate acts, that is, acts not proceeding from human reason and will, for example, digestion or mindlessly stroking one's beard.

Analogical predication—Using the same word twice with meanings, or intelligible contents, that are partly the same and partly different, for example, "The created world is *good*" and "God is *good*."

Articles of faith—Truths revealed by God that human reason unaided by revelation cannot know, for example, the doctrines of the Incarnation or Trinity.

Equivocal predication—Using the same word twice with meanings or intelligible contents that are completely different: for example, "The *bat* flew out of the cave" and "The boy swung the *bat* at the ball."

Essence—What a thing is; expressed in a definition. For example, "man" is defined as a "rational animal," which expresses the essence of "man".

Eternal—Timeless and without succession; only God is *strictly* eternal.

Existence—In Latin, the word *esse*, which means that act that makes a thing be; that act whereby something *is*. For example, this dog exists or *is* because of its *esse*, or act of essence.

Happiness—The ultimate end of human life; human perfection or flourishing, found in its perfect form in the knowledge and love of God in heaven.

Human acts—Free, deliberate acts proceeding from human reason and will; acts over which man is master.

Law—An ordinance of reason promulgated for the common good by the authority in charge of the community.

>**Divine law**—Law directing human beings to heaven as revealed by God in the Old and New Testaments.
>
>**Eternal law**—The eternal plan or conception in God's mind of how all of creation should turn out, by which in particular He providentially directs human beings to their proper, ultimate end, the Beatific Vision in heaven.
>
>**Human law**—Necessary determinations or specifications of the natural law promulgated by the proper authorities that sometimes also have the force of natural law (when they express something found in the natural law), and must never contradict it.
>
>**Natural law**—The rational creature's participation in the eternal law in directing himself toward his ultimate end by the exercise of reason, in accord with the inclinations built into human nature.

Necessary—That which cannot be otherwise, cannot *not* be.

Philosophy—The search for truth, particularly the truth about God, by human reason unaided by God's revelation.

Possible—That which can be otherwise than it is; contingent.

Potency (or potentiality)—What *can be*, as opposed to act or what *is*.

Practical intellect—The human intellect as knowing the truth for sake of acting (or making something). See also *speculative intellect*.

Preambles of faith—Truths (such as God's existence and the immortality of the human soul) that are naturally knowable but are nevertheless revealed by God.

Property—A characteristic of a thing that is not part of its essence but that flows from the essence and is always found in that kind of thing, for example, the ability to laugh in human beings.

Propter quid—A demonstration moving from cause to effect and telling the reason *why* the effect is what it is.

Quia—A demonstration moving from effect to cause, showing *that* the cause exists as the explanation of the effect(s). This is the type of demonstration that applies to proving the existence of God.

Reduction to the absurd—An argument that attacks a position and shows it to be false by pointing out its absurd or impossible consequences.

Soul—The internal source of life for a living thing. See also *substantial form*.

Speculative intellect—The human intellect as knowing the truth simply for the sake of knowing the truth. See also *practical intellect*.

Subsistent—That which exists on its own or independently, not needing to exist *in* something else (though always dependent on God's causality), as opposed to an accident or characteristic (such as, for example, the color red).

Substantial form—An internal principle that makes a thing be the *kind* of thing it is, for example, a horse or a human being; identical to the soul for living things.

Theology—Faith seeking understanding, the rational study of truths revealed by God in an attempt to understand them better.

Univocal predication—Using the same word twice with identical meaning or intelligible content: for example, "The house is *brown*" and "The cow is *brown*."

Vice—A bad operative habit; see also *virtue*.

Virtue—A good operative habit; a perfection of a power that leads to constancy, ease, and pleasure in good action and the attainment of the ultimate end.

Virtue, intellectual—A good operative habit perfecting the intellect either in its speculative or practical operation.

Virtue, moral—A good operative habit perfecting the appetites, including the intellectual appetite, or will, so that the appetites readily obey the dictates of reason.

Virtue, theological—A supernatural gift from God infused into the human soul to allow the human person to know and love God, that is, to exercise a share in God's own life, which is the ultimate end of human life; specifically, faith, hope, and charity (love).

Will—The intellectual appetite; desire consequent upon intellectual knowledge.

FURTHER READING

Aquinas, Thomas. *An Aquinas Reader*. Revised edition. Edited by Mary T. Clark. New York: Fordham University Press, 2000.

Chesterton, G. K. *St. Thomas Aquinas*. San Francisco: Ignatius Press, 2002.

Copleston, F. C. *Aquinas*. London: Penguin, 1955.

Davies, Brian, O.P. *The Thought of Thomas Aquinas*. Oxford: Oxford University Press, 1992.

Kreeft, Peter. *Summa of the* Summa: *The Essential Philosophical Passages of St. Thomas Aquinas'* Summa Theologica *Edited and Explained for Beginners*. San Francisco: Ignatius Press, 1990.

Pieper, Josef. *The Silence of St. Thomas*. Translated by John Murray, S.J., and Daniel O'Connor. South Bend, Ind.: St. Augustine's Press, 1999.

Torrell, Jean-Pierre. *St. Thomas Aquinas*. Volume 1: *The Person and His Work*. Translated by Robert Royal. Washington, D.C.: Catholic University of America Press, 1996.

Wippel, John F. *The Metaphysical Thought of Thomas Aquinas*. Washington, D.C.: Catholic University of America Press, 2000.

INDEX

a priori and a posteriori
   demonstrations of existence of
   God, 7
acts
   extrinsic principles of, 57
   human actions distinguished
      from acts of a man, 35–36,
      79, 80
   potency versus act, 13–14, 79,
      80
analogical predication, 22, 23–24,
   79
Anselm of Canterbury, 6
Aquinas. *See* Thomas Aquinas,
   philosophy of
Aristotle ("the Philosopher")
   on causation, 14
   De Anima, 46
   Ethics, 44, 47–48, 52, 59–60
   on ethics, 36, 44, 45, 46, 47–48,
      52
   on God, 3–4, 14, 16n8
   importance in Thomist thought,
      viii–ix
   on law, 57, 59–60, 68, 70, 73
   Metaphysics, 4, 11, 46, 68, 76
   Physics, 36, 57, 70
   Politics, 47, 48, 59, 73
   Posterior Analytics, 3
   Radical Aristotelians, ix
articles of faith, 3, 24–26, 79
Augustine of Hippo
   Confessions, 42
   De Civitate Dei, 25, 37
   De Doctrina Christiana, 20
   De Libero Arbitrio, 66, 74
   De Trinitate, 27, 42, 44
   Enchiridion, 11–12
   on eternity of world, 25
   on ethics, 37, 42, 44, 48
   on God, 11–12, 20, 25
   on law, 66, 74
   sermon on Psalm 118, 48
   on the soul, 27
   Thomas's use of, viii

beatific vision, 40–41, 45–47, 55
beginning of world as article of
   faith, 24–26
Benedict XVI, ix
Bible and biblical citations. *See*
   Scriptural citations; Scripture

body
    man, as part of definition of, 31–32
    soul, relationship to, 27–28
Boethius, 4, 67
Bradley, Denis J. M., 62*n*1

cardinal virtues, 53–54
causation
    Aristotle on causation, 14
    cause to effect reasoning, 7
    effect to cause reasoning, 7–8
    efficient (first or uncaused) cause, argument from, 10, 14
    infinite regress, concept of, 12–13, 37
charity, as theological virtue, 56. *See also* love
common good, law directed to, 58–60
Confessions (Augustine), 42
contingent or possible being, 15, 80

De Anima (Aristotle), 46
De Bello Gallico (Julius Caesar), 71
De Civitate Dei (Augustine), 25, 37
De Doctrina Christiana (Augustine), 20
De Hebdomadibus (Boethius), 4, 67
De Libero Arbitrio (Augustine), 66, 74
De Trinitate (Augustine), 27, 42, 44
Decalogue, 66–67, 69–70, 72
deliberate human actions, distinguished from acts of a man, 35–36, 79, 80
design, argument from, 11, 17
Dominican order, viii

effect to cause reasoning, 7–8
efficient cause, argument from, 10, 14
Enchiridion (Augustine), 11–12
end-directedness
    existence of God argued from, 11, 17
    of human actions, versus acts of a man, 35–36, 79, 80
    identity of last end for all humans, 39–40
    last or final end of human existence, 36–37
    of man, 35–40
    will entirely directed at last end, 37–38
equivocal predication, 22, 23, 79
essence
    defined, 5, 79
    simplicity of God (identity of essence and existence), 18
eternal law, 61–62, 80
eternity of God alone, 24–26, 79
ethics, 35–56
    end-directedness, 35–40. *See also* end-directedness
    exitus-reditus scheme of *Summa* and, x
    happiness, 40–47. *See also* happiness
    virtue, 47–56. *See also* virtue
Ethics (Aristotle), 44, 47–48, 52, 59–60
Etymologiae (Isidore), 58, 76
evil
    classic answer to problem of, 11–12, 17
    extrinsic principle inclining to, 57

INDEX

natural law as doing good and avoiding evil, 68–70
existence
  defined, 5–6, 79
  identity of existence and essence in God, 18
  inclination to continue in, 33, 69
  of intellectual without moral virtue, 51–53
  of moral without intellectual virtue, 50–51
  soul as subject of, 33
existence of God, 3–17
  demonstrability of, 7–9
  proofs of, 9–17
  as self-evident, 3–6
exitus-reditus scheme of *Summa theologiae*, x
Exodus 3:14, 9
extrinsic principles of acts, 57

faith
  articles of, 3, 24–26, 79
  natural knowledge, relationship to, 8–9
  preambles of, 3, 8, 80
  as theological virtue, 55–56
  theology defined as "faith seeking understanding," 3, 81
  Thomist philosophy embedded in, x
Fallacy of Composition, 15
Fides et Ratio (John Paul II), vii–viii, ix*n*2
final or last end. *See* end-directedness
first cause, argument from, 10, 14
first mover, God as, 9–10, 13–14, 36

First Vatican Council, 8
fortitude, as cardinal virtue, 54
Franciscan order, 43
free will, 41

goal-directedness. *See* end-directedness
God, 1–26
  ability to turn away from, 40–41
  analogical predication about, 22, 23–24, 79
  beginning of world as article of faith, 24–26
  existence of, 3–17. *See also* existence of God
  exitus-reditus scheme of *Summa* and, x
  as extrinsic principle inclining to good, 57
  happiness, as constituting, 40
  infinite goodness of, 11–12, 17
  names of, 19–21, 22
  negative speech about, 19, 22–23
  positive speech about, 19, 22–23
  revelation required for knowledge of, 1–3
  simplicity of (identity of essence and existence), 18
  speech about, 19–24
  truth about God, philosophy as search for, 2, 80
  univocal predication about, 21–22, 23, 81
  will, as ultimate object of, 40
good
  common good, law directed to, 58–60
  created good, happiness not constituted by, 40–41

extrinsic principle inclining to, 57
infinite goodness of God, 11–12, 17
natural law as doing good and avoiding evil, 68–70
virtue as habit of, 48–49, 81
will, universal good as object of, 40
Gregory I the Great, 24

habit, in Thomist sense, 48–49
happiness, 40–47
    as beatific vision, 40–41, 45–47, 55
    cardinal virtues and, 54
    created good not constituting, 40–41
    defined, 80
    law and, 58–59, 60
    as operation of intellect or will, 41–43
    as operation of speculative or practical intellect, 43–45
    theological virtues and, 55
Hebrews 11:1, 6, 24
hope, as theological virtue, 56
human actions, distinguished from acts of a man, 35–36, 79, 80
human law
    defined, 64, 80
    limits to suppression of vice by, 76–77
    natural law and, 65, 74–76
    nature and function of, 64–65
    virtue, as training in, 73–74, 76–77
humanity. *See* intellect; man; soul; will

immortality of soul, 29–31
incorruptibility of soul, 32–33
infinite goodness of God, 11–12, 17
infinite regress, concept of, 12–13, 37
intellect. *See also* reason
    happiness as operation of, 41–43
    incorruptibility of, 32–33
    practical, 43–45, 80
    soul as having, 29, 30–31
    speculative, 43–45, 81
intellectual virtue. *See* virtue
intelligent design, argument from, 11, 17
Isaiah 66:4, 1
Isidore of Seville, 58, 76

John 17:3, 41
1 John 3:2, 46
John Paul II, vii–viii, ix
Julius Caesar, 71
justice, as cardinal virtue, 53, 54

knowledge. *See* faith; intellect; philosophy; reason
Kreeft, Peter, 13*n*6

last or final end. *See* end-directedness
law, 57–77. *See also* human law; natural law
    common good, directed to, 58–60
    competency of reason of any man to make, 59–60
    defined, 61, 80
    divine, 65–67, 80
    eternal, 61–62, 80
    exitus-reditus scheme of *Summa* and, x

Index

happiness and, 58–59, 60
promulgation, necessity of, 60–61
reason, coming from, 57–58
Ten Commandments, 66–67, 69–70, 72
Leo XIII, ix
love
   faith in and love of God, Thomist philosophy embedded in, x
   knowledge versus, 41, 42, 43
   theological virtue, charity as, 56

man. *See also* intellect; will
   end-directedness of, 35–40. *See also* end-directedness
   exitus-reditus scheme of *Summa* and, x
   soul of, 27–33. *See also* soul
Matthew 9:17, 77
maximally great being, argument from, 11, 12, 16–17
Metaphysics (Aristotle), 4, 11, 46, 68, 76
moral virtue. *See* virtues
Moses Maimonides (Rabbi Moses), 19
motion, argument from, 9–10, 13–14, 36

names of God, 19–21, 22
natural law
   commonality of, 70–72
   defined, 63, 80
   as doing good and avoiding evil, 68–70
   human law and, 65, 74–76
   intrinsic to rational creatures, 62–64
   principle precepts of, 67–70
   promulgation of, 61
   self-evidentiary nature of, 67
necessary being, argument from, 10–11, 15–16, 80
negative speech about God, 19, 22–23
Neoplatonism, viii
non-Christian/pagan sources, Thomas's use of, vii–ix

ontological argument, 3–6

pagan/non-Christian sources, Thomas's use of, vii–ix
2 Peter 1:4, 55
"the Philosopher." *See* Aristotle
philosophy. *See also* Thomas Aquinas, philosophy of
   defined, 2, 80
   existence of God demonstrable via, 8
   love versus knowledge, 41, 42, 43
   revelation required as well as, 1–3
Physics (Aristotle), 36, 57, 70
Plato, viii, 31
Politics (Aristotle), 47, 48, 59, 73
positive speech about God, 19, 22–23
possible or contingent being, 15, 80
Posterior Analytics (Aristotle), 3
potency versus act, 13–14, 79, 80
practical intellect, 43–45, 80
practical reason, 70–71
preambles of faith, 3, 8, 80

promulgation of law, necessity of, 60–61
proofs of existence of God, 9–17
property, defined, 43, 81
propter quid philosophical demonstrations, 7, 81
Proverbs
   8:23, 62
   30:33, 77
prudence
   as cardinal virtue, 53, 54
   as intellectual virtue, 50–51
   moral virtue required for, 51–53, 72
Psalms
   52:1 [53:1], 4
   102:5 [103:5], 40
   118, Augustine on, 48

quia philosophical demonstrations, 7–8, 81

Radical Aristotelians, ix
reason. *See also* intellect
   competency of reason of any man to make laws, 59–60
   law coming from, 57–58
   speculative versus practical, 70–71
reduction to the absurd, 15n7, 81
revelation required for knowledge of God, 1–3
Romans 1:20, 7, 8, 22

Scriptural citations
   Exodus 3:14, 9
   Hebrews 11:1, 6, 24
   Isaiah 66:4, 1
   John 17:3, 41
   1 John 3:2, 46
   Matthew 9:17, 77
   2 Peter 1:4, 55
   Proverbs
      8:23, 62
      30:33, 77
   Psalms
      52:1 [53:1], 4
      102:5 [103:5], 40
      118, Augustine on, 48
   Romans 1:20, 7, 8, 22
   2 Timothy 3:16, 1
Scripture
   divine law revealed in, 65–67, 80
   revelation required for knowledge of God, 1–3
   Ten Commandments, 66–67, 69–70, 72
self-evidence
   of existence of God, 3–6
   of natural law principles, 67
sin, as turning away from true last end, 39–41
Socrates, 48, 49
soul, 27–33
   body, relationship to, 27–28
   defined, 81
   identity with man, 31–32
   incorruptibility of, 32–33
   as subsistent or immortal, 29–31, 81
   as substantial form, 28, 81
speculative intellect, 43–45, 81
speculative reason, 70–71
speech about God, 19–24
subsistent nature of soul, 29–31, 81
substantial form, 28, 81

INDEX

Summa contra Gentiles (Thomas Aquinas), 16
Summa theologiae (Thomas Aquinas), vii, x, 1*n*1
syllogisms, 7–8*n*5

Tacelli, Ronald K., 13*n*6
temperance, as cardinal virtue, 53, 54
Ten Commandments, 66–67, 69–70, 72
theological virtues, 55–56
theology, defined, 3, 81
Thomas Aquinas, philosophy of, vii–x
    on ethics, 35–56. *See also* ethics
    faith in and love of God, embedded in, x
    on God, 1–26. *See also* God
    on law, 57–77. *See also* law
    life and thought of Thomas, viii–x
    modern revival of Thomism, ix
    reasons for studying, vii–viii
    on soul, 27–33. *See also* soul
    Summa contra Gentiles, 16
    Summa theologiae, vii, x, 1*n*1
2 Timothy 3:16, 1
truth about God, philosophy as search for, 2, 80

uncaused cause, argument from, 10, 14
understanding, as intellectual virtue, 50, 51
universe's beginning as article of faith, 24–26
univocal predication, 21–22, 23, 81
unmoved mover, God as, 9–10, 13–14, 36

Vatican I, 8
vice, 76–77, 81
virtue, 47–56. *See also* prudence
    cardinal, 53–54
    definitions pertinent to, 48–49, 81, 82
    difference between moral and intellectual virtues, 47–50
    existence of intellectual without moral virtue, 51–53
    existence of moral without intellectual virtue, 50–51
    human law as training in, 73–74, 76–77
    subjects of, 54
    theological, 55–56, 82

will
    defined, 82
    happiness as operation of, 41–43
    last end, entirely directed at, 37–38
    law not primarily from, 58
    universal good as object of, 40
Wippel, John F., 2*n*2
wisdom, defined, 2
world's beginning as article of faith, 24–26

CPSIA information can be obtained at www.ICGtesting.com
Printed in the USA
BVOW08s2155220713

326487BV00006B/14/P